Up From Second Street

The Autobiography
of
California State Senator
Ruben S. Ayala

written by
Ruben S. Ayala

Published by the
Ruben S. Ayala Research Center Library
located in the
**Library of
Ruben S. Ayala
High School**
14255 Peyton Dr. Chino Hills, CA 91709

Edited by Michael Calta

© Copyright 2005 *"Up From Second Street"*
by Ruben S. Ayala

ISBN 0-9761048-9-X

<u>DEDICATION</u>

I dedicate these writings to my wife, Irene, whose patience, understanding and unfaltering love and support have made me a wiser person and a better public servant.

PREFACE

"Up From Second Street" is a project I began upon sensing the need to highlight some of the more meaningful experiences in my life. It is not an all-inclusive personal history, but rather a series of snapshots designed to communicate to the reader the value of those people, principles, places, and events that have meant so much to me. As a child of Mexican heritage growing up in the Chino Barrio in southern California, I had no idea that I would have the opportunity to live the life I have. If I were to describe in one line the formula for living a full life, I think I would borrow the words of the great American sage, Benjamin Franklin, "Doing well by doing good!" When we as individuals cooperate together as families, as teams, as businesses, as congregations, as communities, etc. and commit ourselves to do good for the greater whole, we always do well individually. For that principle, I will always be grateful. Thank you to all, both mentioned and unmentioned, for allowing me to do some good with you!

ACKNOWLEDGEMENTS

To my wife, Irene, my eternal strength. To our loving and faithful sons, Bud, Maurice (*Eddie*) and Gary. To my dad and mom, Mauricio and Herminia Ayala. To my paternal grandparents, Cesario and Inez Ayala. To our devoted Aunt, Esther Martinez. To my brother Maury, for being my early role model. To Marcie Morales, my life-long buddy and fellow veteran of the Marine Corps action in the South Pacific during World War II (WWII). Marcie passed away on April 18, 2003. To Irene's dad and mom, Marcelino and Soledad Morales, for their love and comfort, especially during the early years of our marriage.

To Al McCombs, for his years of support and friendship and his generous time in assisting me in researching the Chino Champion files. To his father, Philip McCombs, who was the first person to suggest that I should write this story. To great coaches in my life, Levi Dickey and Frank Elder. To the man who first encouraged me to run for the Board of Education, Garland Mendenhall. To the Chino Toastmasters Club and the local service clubs for their continual support to me and to their communities.

To Dr. Ken Schofield, Dr. William Aguilar and Dr. Jeff Davis of the Water Resources Institute of Cal State San Bernardino and to Maricarman Ruiz Porras, the Curator of the Ontario Museum, for their support and encouragement of this project. To Michael Calta, for his hard work and expertise in preparing this book for publication. And finally, to all those fine men and women who, without any strings attached, provided the sustained support which allowed me to serve my constituents appropriately for over 43 years. With a sense of indebtedness, I offer a profound "Thank you!"

UP FROM SECOND STREET
by Al McCombs, Publisher-Chino Champion, April 21, 1971

More than 200 friends of the Chairman of the (San Bernardino) County Board of Supervisors gathered last Saturday night to celebrate belatedly a birthday (No. 49), and pay tribute to a great guy.

If you were to ask him today about the next office he aspires to, he would flash his friendly grin and say that he's happy where he is, and very busy. And why not. Three Republicans have a solid hold on the next three offices-Assembly, State Senate and Congress. But after the next redistricting, who knows?

"I did it, and others can too," is the stance Ruben Ayala takes when he hears the old complaint about "lack of opportunity." He'll remind the complainers that he was born in a Mexican Town in Chino and attended the Mexican school, where he and other students got slapped down if they were heard talking Spanish. When he went to the local theater, he and his friends had to enter a separate door and sit in a special section.

But there was one thing that Chino held higher in those days than the separation of nationalities, and that was sports ability. Ruben was blessed with a brother who was a top athlete on some of Chino's best teams in history, and Ruben himself had ability. Cowboy boosters remembered him when he returned from World War II, and this made a difference. But once he got his foot in the door, his successes were his own.

His severest critic is probably his father. "I still don't say no to him," says Mr. Ayala. Mauricio Ayala, Sr. came to the valley over 70 years ago, and to the city of Chino around 1905. He and his wife had six children, five still living, all but one in Chino. Mr. Ayala, now (86), lives quietly and independently in the little house on Second Street where the family grew up. His wife died in 1929, when the youngest were still toddlers, and the grandparents helped raise them. Young Ruben came under two men in high school who had a marked influence on his life. One was his basketball coach, Levi Dickey, later Superintendent of schools. The other was his baseball coach, Frank Elder, then fresh out of La Verne College. It was Ruben's privilege many years later to sign both their contracts as a member of the Board of Education. Then he could kiddingly call Mr. Elder "Frankie," an offense which would cost him a lap around the track in his student days.

A third person he met in high school who affected the course of his life was Irene Morales. "Mother was old fashioned and strict then, and wouldn't let me out of the house," Irene recalls. "So we just met in the halls." Ruben graduated in 1941 and was soon to go off to war as a Marine. He island hopped after Japs in the South Pacific until malaria gained him a ticket stateside. He and Irene were married in 1945. They have three children, Ruben (Buddy), a Vietnam vet now studying for teaching at La Verne; Eddy, studying law at the University of Riverside; and Gary, a Chaffey student. All five members of the family are Chino High grads.

Ruben Ayala might have been fixing television sets today if he had kept his interest in electronics after graduating from the National School in Los Angeles (close enough to USC to claim the Trojans for his own). But he turned instead to insurance, which provided him with an opportunity to meet people, and the gregarious Mr. Ayala was good at this. His entry into politics was in the school board election in 1955, at the urging of his friend Garland Mendenhall, now principal at Los Serranos. He hasn't lost an election since.

He spent two terms on the board, then ran for city council, and got the top vote. It was closer in 1964 when he became Chino's first elected mayor serving here two years before taking on incumbent county supervisor Paul Young. "The days of the horse and buggy type of representation are over," he said in his campaign, and the majority of voters agreed.

He soon gained country wide attention. He was forthright and tough. At one point he and a fellow supervisor resisted bureaucracy and hammered out an austerity budget to keep the tax rate down, when other supervisors found reason to be absent. Minority group representatives howled when he forced the county war on poverty organization to reform and become more effective. Later, as chairman of the board, he gained the reputation as the "fastest gavel in the west," having been conditioned several years before as an occasionally confused president of the parliamentary-bent Chino Toastmasters Club.

He has taken on the sheriff, the district attorney and the judges, heretofore the "untouchables" of San Bernardino County government. He may have made some enemies, but he also gained a lot of friends among the little people who are glad to know that there is somebody up there who won't be pushed around. He also has the respect of county employees who like a strong chief executive officer.

Ruben Ayala will probably never equal the four terms of his predecessor. It would be a waste if he did. There are better things in store for the well digger's son with the friendly smile and the fast gavel.

SAN BERNARDINO COUNTY
RESOLUTION
(circa 1974)

Whereas, Ruben Ayala, having been born and raised in the City of Chino,

and, whereas, even in his early childhood showed potential of leadership when he was known as "Swish" on the basketball court and having proven himself as a leader in the athletic field,

and, whereas, upon reaching adulthood and having trained himself as a television engineer and insurance agent, he pursued a career in these occupations until such time as the people of Chino, finding their tv's in ill-repair and the insurance rates rising, sought for him a new vocation and elected him to the Chino Unified School District Board of Education,

and, whereas, shortly afterwards, the people recognizing that they had made a grave error, immediately convinced him to run for the city council of the City of Chino to which he was overwhelmingly elected,

and, whereas, they again recognized the mistake they had made and looking for some other place to send him, they elected him as a Supervisor from the 4th Supervisorial District to represent them in county government,

and, whereas, at this point, not only had they gotten him out of the city, but at the same time, had shoved the responsibility of what to do with him into the hands of four other Supervisors;

and, whereas, these four Supervisors found that he was such a problem, that they unanimously made him Chairman of the Board of Supervisors where they could keep their eye on him;

and, whereas, in hopes that he would change his checkered sports coat, these supervisors elected him to a second consecutive term as Chairman of the Board;

and, whereas, failing in this and in final desperation, knowing not where to send him, they suggested that he would be much better off as a Senator in Sacramento;

and, whereas, having won the election to the State Senate, everyone's prayers having been answered, Ruben Ayala, continues to live up to a reputation of creating problems;

and, whereas, it appears that it is only a matter of time until his colleagues will be lending their help to get him elected to a statewide office;

now therefore be it resolved, that having polled all the people who have been associated with him through his career, and having found that each of the people associated with him have affirmed the statements above, we, the Board of Supervisors of San Bernardino County, adopt this resolution by default.

Bob, Jim, Dennis, Joe, Bob

Bob Hammock
Jim Mayfield
Dennis Hansberger
Joe Kamansky
Bob Townsend

THE BOY WHO DIDN'T KNOW ALL THE WORDS
By John Jopes, Columnist, Daily Bulletin,
(circa July 28, 1993 - printed as published)

When Ramon Valdez was just a boy he lived in Chino and played in the dusty streets of the barrio.

The word "barrio" probably wasn't used much in those days, for it had yet to become a popular term.

His family was poor, but Ramon didn't realize it because in the Great Depression days of the "30's" there was nothing much with which to compare poverty. The whole town was poor.

There was little to covet because there was a certain sameness to everyone's lot in life. And everyone's lot was not much.

Ramon's family was close, as were most poor families of that time. The hunt for survival in those days did that to families.

The boy's father was proud and hard-working. Through all of the Depression he was never on welfare (or relief as they called it then), nor was he ever employed by the WPA or any other government agency.

He drilled water wells around southern California and was away from home much of the time.

Ramon's father was stern, but infinitely fair with his children, and he taught Ramon that if he were true to himself he would be true to everyone.

The advice became the guidon that Ramon followed the rest of his life. The mark of that paternal lesson remains on him to this day.

When Ramon was 5 years old his mother died, and he was raised by his grandparents.

Although the older couple lived in Chino, they were both born in Mexico, and were still tethered strongly to their Mexican heritage and their Mexican ways.

Neither spoke English very well.

Ramon's environment rendered him bilingual when he was just a child.

His mother had spoken English well. But because she was gone from Ramon's life, and his father was away so often, the Spanish language became a dominant part of Ramon's world.

One day at grammar school, Ramon's teacher wrote "adventure" on the blackboard and instructed the youngsters in her class to write a short composition based on the word.

The essay was to be turned in a few days later.

Ramon did not know what "adventure" meant. He did not, in fact, know what "composition" meant.

He felt lost and embarrassed.

When the day arrived for the children to turn in their work, Ramon had nothing to submit.

He was devastated.

The teacher kept him after school - not to punish him, but to ask him why he had not written his composition.

He told her his story, and said he was sure he could have done the work if he had known what the words meant.

Ramon, who has been a good friend of mine for more than 30 years, told me this story at lunch the other day while we spoke of many things. It was that childhood incident, he said, that makes him favor bilingual education.

Surely, he said he believes bilingual education would serve as the quickest way to help kids learn the English language.

Why should a child suffer in his studies, he said, because he is not familiar with English and has no one at home who can help him or no one at home who cares?

It's not fair to the children, he said. It's only right to help them in school.

He said bilingual schooling should have nothing to do with ethnic relationships. All of us are, after all, Americans, Ramon said to me.

"It's something like when I was a Marine in the war," he said.

"Nobody ever called me a Mexican Marine. I was a U.S. Marine, just like all my buddies.

"We were just trying to help one another stay alive."

"Helping each other learn is something like that," he said.

By the way, Ramon is not my friend's real name.

His real name is Ruben.

Ruben Ayala.

California State Senator Ruben S. Ayala.

California State Senator Ruben S. Ayala 1974-1998

"Up From Second Street"   Ruben S. Ayala

TABLE OF CONTENTS

CHAPTER ONE

MI HERENCIA

My story begins with my beloved paternal grandparents, Cesario and Inez Ayala. Migrating from the State of Durango in Mexico to the Chino Valley in southern California in 1900, they arrived ten years before the City of Chino was incorporated. Chino became my birthplace on March 6, 1922.

My mother died when I was around six years old and Dad moved my brother, Maury, my three sisters, Susie, Stella and Rosina, and me to my grandparents' home. It was up the same street near the corner of 2nd and D Street in Chino, California. Dad was away working much of the time and wanted us to have a stable upbringing. I lived there until I joined the U.S. Marines in 1942. Growing up in my grandparents' home, I knew them well and have grown to appreciate them even more now as I enjoy my later years.

Second Street was a great place to grow up. Everyone knew each other and I always felt like I was among family and friends. My wife, Irene, grew up on the corner of 5th and D street. The living conditions were tight, but we didn't know any better back then. It was like that for everyone, at least everyone we knew.

There were ten of us in that small converted three-bedroom house on 2nd Street - five adults and five children. Along with my grandparents and my father, my Aunt Clara and Uncle Anastacio lived with us. We just made the best of it.

However, it was a segregated neighborhood back then, known as the Chino Barrio. It was the most densely populated of the few areas in town where people of Mexican heritage were allowed to live. Monte Vista, which used to be 1st Street, was the neighborhood's western border. 5th Street was the eastern border and Riverside and Chino Avenues were the northern and southern borders, respectively. We didn't have any sidewalks or gutters back then and the streets weren't paved. It wasn't much different than a neighborhood you might see today in Tijuana, Mexico.

My grandmother, Inez, was a tough "ol' gal" - a strong disciplinarian. My dad took after her on that score. My grand-dad, Cesario, was more easy-going, but he had a strong work ethic. My father inherited his hard-working nature and was a great example to me.

When my grandparents crossed the Mexican border into El Paso, Texas in early 1900, my granddad sent my grand-ma and their children (my Aunt Clara, my Aunt Rosa and my father, Mauricio, who was just a youth) ahead to Chino, California where they had friends. My granddad and my Uncle Anastacio, who suffered from severe back problems, then worked their way to southern California as laborers on the rail-road. Arriving in Ontario, California later on that year, they walked the last six miles to Chino for a very satisfying reunion with their family and friends.

Granddad and Grandma Ayala were farm workers during the spring and summer. They also chopped wood in the summer, which they sold during the winter. I remember riding with my Granddad Ayala on a horse and wagon on Edison Ave. in Chino to deliver cords of wood to customers living at "El

Campo de Almanza." It was a camp of itinerant farm workers
and their families located where the California Institution for
Men is today. This was during the Great Depression of the
1930's. Even farm work was hard to come by then. Folks
migrating from the Dust Bowl, mainly from Oklahoma and
Arkansas, where they had been plagued by severe drought and
crop devastating dust storms, the worst in U.S. history, were
competing for the same limited job opportunities as the local
workers.

      I remember my grandparents' home didn't have electric-
ity or natural gas, so we didn't have hot running water while
growing up. A wood-burning stove and kerosene lamps were
the best we had. Everything else was improvised. It was a time
of great scarcity, but it was our home and for the time and circumstance, it was our plenty.

      Unfortunately, I didn't know my maternal grandfather.
My mother's parents were from Sonora, Mexico. My
Grandfather Martinez died there, leaving behind my grandmother, Dolores Martinez, my mother, Herminia, and her sister, my Aunt Esther. After his death around 1905, they migrat-
ed to Chino, California to live with friends. I vaguely remember
my Grandma Martinez passing away when I was a young child.

      My recollections of my mother, Herminia, are also few.
She was in her early thirties when she passed away in 1929. I
understand she died following an appendectomy operation.
Something went wrong. Medical science has come a long way
since then. I do remember how musically talented my mother
was. She was a fine organist. One image vividly comes to
mind. I remember watching her set out empty glasses of the
same size and filling each with water to different levels. She
would then strike each glass with a spoon, adjust the water levels to get the proper note and arrange them in line according to
scale. With her spoon, glass, and water ensemble readied, and

her hallmark gentility, she would entertain us with her favorite beautiful tunes. While I inherited her appreciation for music, I was not fortunate enough to inherit her special talent for creating it.

My father, as a young man not yet married, learned the trade of sinking and installing water wells. He learned the trade from a gentleman whose name was Tony Olson. He was the owner of a Chino-based water-drilling company. They drilled wells on Native American reservations in Arizona. Later on, my father worked for water drilling firms servicing the farming communities in the Chino Valley and throughout southern California.

From his visits to Arizona, Dad brought home some beautiful Native American-made rugs. My favorite one was a rug with a broad border. I liked to use the wide border as a road for my toy cars. That hobby kept me entertained for many hours, especially during the rainy season.

In 1929, Dad was working for Mike De Young in the water drilling business. At the time, Mr. De Young decided to buy a new Dodge, four-door sedan. According to Dad, Mr. De Young could get a deal he couldn't turn down if he bought two new Dodge sedans. Each car would cost around $500. Mr. De Young approached Dad with a bargain of his own. If Dad bought the second car, then Mr. De Young promised him that he would have a job with him for as long as he was paying for the new car. Having assurances of a steady job meant more to my father than the new car. On the strength of a handshake, the deal was consummated. Mr. De Young, to his credit, kept his word.

Dad later worked for Joe Brinderson and Frank Mogle, both in the water drilling business. Brinderson Hall at the Chino Fair Grounds was named in honor of Joe Brinderson for his many years of service to the community. Frank Mogle later served as a San Bernardino County Supervisor during WWII, representing the 4th District.

As the Depression worsened, Dad's work steadily dwindled. To supplement the family's income, Dad didn't have any problem working in the fields as a laborer. He did what he had to do to provide for his family as long as it was honest work. He was a strict disciplinarian with a strong work ethic. He was a responsible breadwinner. Dad passed away in 1981 at the age of ninety-six.

Before his passing, Irene and I stopped in to visit him at the Chino Valley Medical Center. We were returning from a Rialto City Council meeting where we were presented with a replica of the actual Rialto street sign dedicated to our name, "Ayala Drive." The street runs north to south from North Riverside Avenue in Rialto to Baseline Road in Rialto where Ayala Drive then changes into Cedar Avenue.

My father was so pleased to have a street sign officially bearing our family name. The last photograph we have of him is in his hospital bed with his arms wrapped around "Ayala Drive." It was a beautiful evening for all of us. Thank you, Dad, for so much!

Aunt Esther, my mother's younger sister, never married. I believe she felt it was her responsibility to help take care of us after my mother's passing. She was an angel to us and to many others. She was our moral compass, always encouraging us to do well in school and motivating us to go to church.

In offering her eulogy, the Reverend Victor Tejera, spoke of how welcome she had made him feel when he had first begun his ministry years prior. He told the gathering how nervous and unsure he was on his first Sunday and how Aunt Esther approached him and in the kindest and warmest way assured him that everything would be fine and that he wasn't alone. She assured him that she and the others in the congregation were there to support him. Aunt Esther was always there for others.

My Aunt Esther was also a remarkable seamstress. She made most of my sisters' clothes as they were growing up. When they needed a dress for a special occasion, she would take them with her and go window-shopping. They would search and search the display windows until they found just the right dress for the occasion. Aunt Esther would carefully study the chosen style and make a series of mental sketches. Once satisfied, they would return home and Aunt Esther would immediately cut the pattern for the dress using newspaper. On a later shopping trip, the right material would be purchased and after some time diligently sewing, Aunt Esther would create beautiful looking dresses for my sisters. When I was in high school, she made me a smart looking sports blazer. It fit perfectly and I wore it with pride. Despite our scarce resources growing up, Aunt Esther always made sure the Ayala children were taken care of.

Aunt Esther worked for twenty years as a forelady at the Della Robbia Wreath-making operation at Boys Republic. Established in 1907, Boys Republic is a working farm and treatment community for troubled youth located on 200 acres in Chino Hills. The organization has helped over 23,000 at risk youth transform themselves into productive individuals. Actor Steve McQueen is one of their more famous success stories.

Boys Republic founder, Margaret Fowler, founded the Della Robbia Wreath program in 1923. According to Boys Republic Director, Max Scott, "Mrs. Fowler had the youngsters in her care make Christmas wreaths as a way for them to earn money for craft projects and to stay busy during the holidays. Within a few years, the wreaths became so popular that they became a source of self-help funding for the school as well."

Every year a specially prepared giant Della Robbia Wreath is sent to the White House to adorn our nation's home during the holidays. Aunt Esther's creativity, strong work ethic, bilingual skills, and most importantly, her genuine concern for others, contributed much to the success of the Della Robbia Wreath program at Boys Republic. Today, the Della Robbia Wreath program generates around $2 million annually. These vital funds make a tremendous difference in the lives of hundreds of young men, as they work to improve their lives.

On her 100th birthday, I called Aunt Esther from my Sacramento Office. By then, I was a retired State Senator and serving on the California Unemployment Insurance Board. She told me how pleased she was that I had remembered her birthday. We reminisced a bit before she asked me, "Where are you calling me from?" Thinking she would be further pleased, I told her I was calling from the State Capital. She immediately admonished me that I should not be using a government phone for personal phone calls and to go to my own home and call her from there. That was my Aunt Esther, compassionate in her own giving, conservative in the government's.

Having contributed so much, Aunt Esther passed away in the year 2000 at the age of one hundred. Her life was a great contribution to us all.

One very happy day which left a lasting impression on me was when Grandma Ayala took us children to a Fourth of July celebration at the Chino Park, bordered by Central Avenue, Ninth Street, D Street and Chino Avenue. I was around eight years old. We were all dressed in our Sunday best. My outfit was a white sailor's suit with cap and all. The parade marched south on Central Avenue. The band played patriotic music and the World War I veterans marched in their uniforms. American flags were seen everywhere. The civic leaders gave discourses about patriotism and civic duty.

What I remember most vividly about that day, however, is that Grandma Ayala bought each of us an ice cream cone. Typical of an eight-year-old, I spilled some ice cream on my nice white outfit. Although Grandma Ayala didn't scold me, I must have felt guilty for letting my grandma down, because I still remember the day so clearly.

My father, mother and Aunt Esther spoke English, but my grandparents did not. They spoke Spanish. Since Dad was away working a lot, we were usually under the supervision of our grandparents. Consequently, when I started grade school, I hadn't learned English yet. The Chino schools in those days were segregated. The D Street School was located where D street ends in the Chino Barrio at Monte Vista. The site is currently Monte Vista Park. Children of Mexican heritage were assigned to this school. None of the teachers could speak Spanish and most of the students didn't know English.

I would guess that 99% of the D Street students did not integrate with "non-Mexican" students until the 7th grade, when they were transferred to Chino Junior High School. It was located on the western campus of Chino High School, which was located where the Chino Valley Unified School District's administration parking lot is today. During segregation, children of Mexican heritage would have to travel outside their neighborhood elementary schools in order to attend the school site in the Chino Barrio designated for them. Segregation made it more difficult for Mexican-American students to gain an appropriate education. The end result of the Chino School District's segregation policy was that, by design, it created a distinctly disadvantaged ethnic group of students. I never dreamed in those days as a young segregated Mexican-American student that years later I would return as a member of the Chino Board of Education, to help assure that attitudes and policy never reverted back to the degrading and humiliating practice of segregation.

Superintendent Levi H. Dickey deserves a lot of credit for pursuing the desegregation of Chino elementary schools. He was a WWII Navy veteran and had previously been my Chino High basketball and football coach, math instructor and

Vice Principal of Chino High School. Levi Dickey had a difficult time convincing some Chino residents that it was time to end segregation. Many of Chino's prominent families were against any change to the policy. Despite the personal cost, Levi Dickey and his supporters prevailed. He once told me, disappointedly, that he had lost some friends over the issue. However, he held steadfast to his belief that there should be equality in education for all of Chino School District's students. In my opinion, Levi Dickey was an effective classroom teacher, a highly successful coach and one of the most outstanding Superintendents in the history of Chino schools. In honor of his successful and worthwhile efforts, a Chino Unified School District elementary school was named the Levi H. Dickey Elementary School in 1980. Levi H. Dickey Elementary School opened its doors to students in 1981 and it remains a tribute to the ideal of ethnic equality in education to this day.

As an elementary school student, I distinctly remember three historical national and international events. Miss Olson, my kindergarten teacher, with obvious pride and admiration, told our class about Charles A. Lindbergh's heroic solo flight across the Atlantic Ocean from New York to France in a single-engine airplane covering 3600 miles in 33½ hours. The year was 1927 and Mr. Lindbergh was the first person to accomplish the feat. I remember us playing "Lindy the Aviator" during recess on the playground.

Another significant event took place in 1931. My fourth-grade teacher, Mrs. Pearl Smith, who later became our son Maurice's 3rd grade teacher, announced that Thomas A. Edison, one of the greatest inventors of all time, had passed away. I was old enough to remember that two of Mr. Edison's many inventions included the electric light bulb and the motion picture machine. As I grew older, I further realized how dramatically Mr. Edison's inventions and discoveries had and would affect our lives. From radio to television, movies to telecommunications and on through the digital age, Thomas A. Edison has laid an impressive and incomparable legacy through his ingenious and prolific endeavors.

My favorite story about Thomas Edison is told by his son, Charles Edison, in the biography he wrote about his father, "The Electric Thomas Edison."

Charles recounts, "One December evening the cry of 'FIRE!' echoed through the plant. Spontaneous combustion had broken out in the film room. Within moments all the packing compounds, celluloid for records, film and other flammable goods had gone up with a whoosh … When I couldn't find father, I became concerned. Was he safe? With all his assets going up in smoke, would his spirit be broken? He was 67, no age to begin anew. Then I saw him in the plant yard, running toward me. 'Where's Mom?' he shouted. 'Go get her' Tell her to get her friends! They'll never see a fire like this again.'

"At 5:30 the next morning, when the fire was barely under control, he called his employees together and announced, 'We're rebuilding.' One man was told to lease all the machine shops in the area. Another, to obtain a wrecking crane from the Erie Railroad Company. Then, almost as an afterthought he added, 'Oh by the way. Anybody know where we can get some money?' Later on he explained, 'You can always make capital out of disaster. We've just cleared out a bunch of old rubbish. We'll build bigger and better on these ruins.' With that he rolled up his coat for a pillow, curled up on a table and immediately fell asleep."

Inspired by people such as Thomas Edison, I learned how to build a crystal radio set at around eleven years old. It was a radio with a quartz crystal that didn't require electricity. Necessary, however, was a long high-wire antenna strung out between two locations with lightning arresters. Edward "Ed"

Carbajal, who was one year ahead of me in school, helped me build my first crystal set. Ed was one of those self-taught Jack-of-all-trades.

Earphones were expensive, so I had just one set. Once in a while, a member of my family would put on the earphones and listen to the only radio station we could receive, KFI. One night in 1936, after everyone had gone to sleep, I remember listening to the coronation ceremony of England's King George VI. The reception was sometimes fuzzy, but in my mind it was as if I were actually there.

The third event took place in 1932. Our fifth grade teacher, Charlotte Hoover, announced the results of the 1932 U.S. Presidential election. Franklin D. Roosevelt had defeated incumbent Herbert C. Hoover. Afterwards, I remember seeing automobiles carrying spare tires above their rear bumpers with the slogan, "Goodbye, Hoover." Franklin Roosevelt was still President ten years later when I joined the Marines in 1942.

In 1935, I was advanced to Chino Junior High School. It was the only junior high school in the district at the time. At least fifty students were promoted to the seventh grade, but, as I can recall, only four of us finally graduated from Chino High School in June of 1941. Still suffering from the Great Depression, many children were forced to drop out of school to go to work in order to help sustain their families. I was fortunate to have been able to graduate.

When I entered Chino Junior High School, I was integrated for the first time with "non-Mexican" students. At first, it was rather intimidating to sit in class with all of these kids with fair skin and many with blonde hair. However, it didn't take me long to assimilate, partly because my brother was already becoming the school athletic hero. He would later become a champion athlete for Chino High School. I discovered that making new friends came rather easily for me. I began to have lunch with some of my new friends. An

opportunity soon presented itself. Since the walk home was
too far to be able to go home for lunch, my grandma or Aunt
Clara would pack me a lunch. One day, I was sitting on the
football field bleachers, eating my lunch with my new friends,
when I reluctantly unpacked one of my everyday tacos. One of
my new friends, Geoffrey Ayres, took notice and asked, "What
is that?"

"Just a taco," I told him. My tacos were like today's
burritos. I guess my friend had never seen one. He wanted to
know if he could have a bite. After sharing half, he asked me if
on the next day I would trade one of my tacos for one of his
peanut butter and jelly sandwiches. That was just fine with me.
I liked peanut butter and jelly and we rarely had it at home.
Well, the word soon spread that Ruben had a delicious Mexican
sandwich for lunch everyday and he was willing to trade.
Before the year was over, I was trading one of my tacos for
three peanut butter and jelly sandwiches. Pretty good exchange
rate, I thought.

There were other opportunities I noticed during my
early years. When I was nine or ten years old, I built my own
shoeshine box. I attached a leather strap to it so I could hang it
over my shoulder. With my dad's help, I purchased the necessary shoe polishing materials and with his permission, on
Saturday nights, I joined some older friends and we shined
shoes. Dances were held at the old Opera House, located on
the southwest corner of Seventh and D Streets, where the City
Hall now sits. We charged ten cents for the shoeshine and
hoped for a nickel tip. Usually, after I had earned at least a dollar, I would go to Reutgen's Bakery, located on Sixth Street
across from where the Chino Youth Museum is now located.
With my hard earned dollar, I would buy fresh baked goods for
the family to enjoy on Sunday morning.

Many years ago, a shipping warehouse for the Chino
Valley Walnut Growers was located on the north side of Chino

Avenue, just west of Monte Vista. In the moving of huge volumes of walnuts, invariably, some walnuts would be damaged and considered inappropriate for market. The damaged walnuts would be disposed of in piles behind the building. Often, with permission, I would sift through the piles and pick out the clean, still healthy walnut meat. It would take me a while, but I would gather about a pound of good walnuts. I bargained with Reutgen's Bakery and exchanged the pound of good walnuts for whatever kind of bread I wanted to take home. Reutgen's Bakery and I had a great relationship during my young entrepreneurial years.

　　　Looking back, I can see how useful these experiences were for me. They prepared me to recognize opportunities and make good use of them for the benefit of those around me. It wasn't anything I had to really think about. Finding and making good use of opportunities for myself and others just seemed to come naturally.

"Up From Second Street"   Ruben S. Ayala

CHAPTER TWO

EARLY IMPRESSIONS

I have always been grateful for my Mexican-American heritage, despite the difficulties it has sometimes attracted. One annoying and unforgettable incident, that to this day remains an irritation, occurred when I was walking home one evening from studying at the local county branch library. The library was located on D Street, just west of 7th street in Chino. I was wearing my high school letterman's sweater and carrying my books under my arm. As I drew near the corner of 2nd and D Streets, half a block from my house, the red light from a police car lit up behind me. The policeman ordered me to stop. Stepping out of his car, he shined his flashlight right in my face. He ordered me to give him my name and demanded to know from where I was walking. I respectfully answered his questions. He demanded I show him my identification. I pulled out my wallet and was reaching into it for my identification when he snatched the wallet out of my hands. He threw the contents, one piece at a time, onto the ground. Once emptied, he tossed my wallet into the gutter. Still shining his flashlight in my face, he snapped at me, "Now pick up your trash and get the hell on home." Years later, when I became the Mayor of Chino, I went looking for this poor imitation of a peace officer. By then, he was nowhere to be found.

My grandparents were able to save enough money for down payments on several parcels of land in the Chino Barrio.

The local establishment was adept at assuring that the Chino Barrio, also known as the Colonia, was the only area in town where people of Mexican heritage could acquire real estate. The same racist mentality existed when I came home after my four-year tour of duty with the Marines after World War II. A Chino real estate agent refused to show my wife and me any properties outside the Chino Barrio. The year was 1950.

A noteworthy annual event of my early years was the celebration of Las Fiestas Patrias, organized by the Colonia's leaders. It was a patriotic festival on the 16th of September, Mexico's Independence Day, celebrating independence after 300 years of Spanish rule. The festivities were held on 6th Street, south of D Street. I recall many folks gathered in their neighbors' homes to make the green, white and red streamers, representing Mexico's national colors. The streamers were suspended about twenty feet high across 6th Street. A wooden platform was constructed and used as a stage. There was a parade and, of course, the Mexican Independence Queen was selected.

The night before, at the Chino High School auditorium, Mexican patriotic speeches were made and at midnight, a dignitary would give the traditional Grito de Dolores. This was the cry given by the then obscure priest, Miguel Hidalgo, when he urged his Indian followers to drive out their Spanish rulers in 1810. It has been said that the peal of Hidalgo's church bell in Mexican history forever rings with the peal of the Liberty Bell in U.S. history. It has also been said that Father Hidalgo is Mexico's George Washington, while Benito Juarez is Mexico's Abraham Lincoln.

All along 6th street, there were Mexican musicians, food, folk dancing and other kinds of merrymaking filled the street. Couples, young and old, danced in the street throughout the night. From time to time, someone would venture to the microphone and offer some affectionate words about their Mexican culture and heritage. One of the highlights was watching the Basque dancers in their colorful costumes perform their cherished cultural dances. The most memorable dances were La Jota and El Jarabe Tapatio (Mexican hat dance). These unforgettable fiestas were organized by the proud, hardworking men and women, who wished to commemorate the struggles and valiant accomplishments of the Mexican people. Chino's diversity was evident as local Swiss, French and French Basque, Spanish Basque, Asians, Italians and Portuguese joined in the celebration.

In 1938, my oldest sister, Susie, and my brother, Maury, graduated from Chino High School. I had just finished my freshman year. Maury is still considered one of the greatest all-around athletes in the history of Chino High School. He is the only athlete I know of who received five letters in one sport, in just four years. As a freshman, he played with the B Basketball Team and earned his B letter. The same year, the varsity team won the Tri-County League title and entered the California Interscholastic Federation (CIF) Tournament. Coach Levi Dickey drafted Maury to play with the varsity team. The ruling at that time was if you entered a game during a CIF tournament, you automatically lettered in that sport. Maury not only played in the game, but he made an impression with his remarkable ability, gaining the attention of reporters. Maury received two letters in basketball as a freshman and three more varsity basketball letters over the next three years.

Maury also received all-league honors as the quarterback who led the Chino High "Cowboy" football team to the Tri-County League Championship in 1937. Freshman Marcie Morales, Irene's brother, was Maury's substitute. That year, the Cowboys played all of the Tri-County League games without being scored on. The Chino High football team, after winning the league championship, played Santa Barbara High at Santa Barbara, California. The Cowboy Special train to Santa Barbara was full to capacity with Chino fans. We ended up losing the game, but the whole experience was definitely worth the ride.

As a baseball player, Maury pitched four no-hitters in high school. He also ran the high hurdles and threw the shot put in track. He was also an outstanding tennis player.

Maury was a senior when I was a freshman and like him I played several sports. My brother's senior class was loaded with gifted athletes. When they graduated, they left a void that we underclassmen were expected to fill. Eventually, as seniors, we were able to meet their mark, but we struggled in the years prior. Frank Elder was our baseball coach. He had a rule that for every bad decision or error made by a player during practice, the player would have to run around the track one time. As sophomores, we didn't win as many games as we wanted, but after running around the track as many times as we did, we were the best-conditioned team in the league. The Chino High School basketball gym was later appropriately named the Frank Elder Gym.

Maury went on to play professional baseball as a pitcher for the L.A. Angels in the Pacific Coast League. He is an alumnus of Humboldt State College and lives with his wife, Kay, and their three sons in Eureka, California.

When I was in high school, I wanted so much to be like my big brother, Maury. He was my stimulus for wanting to raise the bar and achieve the very best I could. His example instilled within me a burning desire to be a winner. Later on, that winning impulse would be galvanized in the Marine Corps, although under much more hostile circumstances.

Inspired to emulate my brother, as a high school sophomore, I earned the varsity baseball team's highest batting average trophy. In my junior and senior years, I was an all tournament selection at the La Verne, Huntington Beach and Chino basketball tournaments. I earned all Tri-County League honors and was the league's second highest scorer. Ross Dana, Jr. from Citrus High School was the league's top scorer that year. Ross

Dana, Sr., Ross's father, later served as a County Supervisor from the desert region during my time on the San Bernardino County Board of Supervisors.

I was also honored when my teammates selected me captain of our team. My name was placed on a large blanket-size banner along with the names of the most valuable players of each sport for the year. The perpetual banner was kept at the school and a smaller replica was awarded to the athlete.

Another early role model of mine was Sef Murillo, who preceded my brother as an outstanding athlete at Chino High School. Sef went on to San Diego State College, where he was a standout in basketball. After serving in the U.S. Army during World War II, he returned to San Diego State College and graduated with a Bachelor's Degree in Education. Sef retired as Principal of Point Loma High School in San Diego and was recently inducted into the San Diego State College Basketball Hall of Fame.

Most of my fellow high school athletes have passed away. My closest buddy was Marcie Morales. We were so close that we even joined the Marine Corps together. It was because of my close friendship with Marcie that I met my future wife, his sister, Irene. I was a sophomore and Irene was a freshman when we first met in 1939. I was a budding athlete and Irene was an academic, later becoming a life member of the California Scholastic Federation (CSF). In her senior year, she was editor of the school newspaper and won the Outstanding Girl Athlete Award. Irene later graduated from Chaffey College and the California Hospital School of Nursing and was a member of the U.S. Cadet Nurse Corps. She went on to earn her Bachelor of Science Degree in Nursing from the University of Southern California. We were married on July 22, 1945.

Besides school, sports and spending time with family and friends, like most teens, I needed to work. One summer, I drove my Aunt Clara and other ladies to work at the Stewart-

Ryder Dry Yard in Dad's 1929 Dodge. The dry yard was located on the east side of Ontario Road between Chino Avenue
and Riverside Drive. The ladies worked under a shed, slicing
apricots and peaches in half and removing the pits. They
would stand on both sides of long picnic-sized tables and
spread the cut fruit onto trays. They were paid for each box of
fruit they processed. The men would then place the trays of
cut fruit in sulfur huts for the night. The next morning the
trays of fruit would be removed and spread out in an open field
to dry in the hot summer sun. After driving the ladies to work,
I usually stayed to help my aunt.

One morning, Bert Ryder, one of the owners, came
over to the shed where I was helping my Aunt cut apricots and
said to me, "Hey, Kid, do you want to work out with the men?"
Apparently, one of the men had gone home sick. I jumped at
the chance. I worked the rest of that summer spreading and
picking up trays of fruit. The men were paid 12 cents an hour.
When we worked 10 hours, under the hot sun, we earned $1.20
and were grateful to have a job. I saved enough money that
summer to buy all of my school clothes for the following year.
I recall that a good pair of shoes cost around $5.00 and one
gallon of gasoline was 11 cents. Milk shakes were 5 cents.

In the late 1930's, the American Beet Sugar Company
continued to own and farm much of the land in the Chino
Valley between the triangular shaped boundaries of Euclid Ave.
and the present Chino Valley Freeway (HWY 71, then known
as South Garey Ave.), with Schaefer Ave. as the northern border and the third leg of the triangle. Richard Gird, an early
Chino pioneer, built the first sugar beet processing factory in
Chino in 1890 with the backing of the Oxnard brothers, the
owners of the American Beet Sugar Company. Through his
vision and industry, Richard Gird is credited for transforming
Chino from El Rancho del Chino into the Township of Chino,
laying the groundwork for Chino's incorporation in 1910.

"Up From Second Street"   Ruben S. Ayala

When I was 17 years old, I worked topping sugar beets where the California Institution for Men is located today. It was the most physically demanding work I ever did. To top sugar beets, we straddled each row of beets in a stooping position while the hot summer sun seared our backs. Using a machete with a slightly bent spike at the end of the blade, we hooked a sugar beet already displaced from the ground by a disc plow, brought it towards us, cut off the green foliage and threw the topped beets to our left in a row, ready to be loaded. Our only break in the arduous repetition was to load the truck each time it returned from unloading at the Chino Sugar Beet processing factory, located west of where Centro Basco restaurant is today on Central Avenue. From the processing plant, others loaded the sugar beets into gondola type train cars for an overnight trip to the Oxnard Sugar Beet Factory.

After bending over all day, it was difficult to stand straight. Yet, a few hours later, after showering and having dinner, I would be playing softball with friends under the lights at the Chino High baseball field. Morales Market, owned by Irene and Marcie's parents, was our team sponsor.

In contrast, one of my easiest jobs was working at Los Serranos Country Club as a caddy. I was still in junior high and would walk the four to five miles each way for my weekend duties. Golf carts were not yet available. As a caddy, I was the golf cart. Caddying paid relatively well. In a few hours, I could take home more money than working all day in the fields. The going rate for caddying was $1 for carrying one player's golf bag and $2.50 if you carried clubs for two players. The older and more experienced caddies received preferential treatment from the caddy master, Zeke "Peanuts" Fajardo. They knew the better players and which players tipped more generously. Many of the older caddies had established a good rapport with the better players and simply waited for them to check in with the caddy master. The younger caddies were assigned to the

leftovers. Most of the players turned down by the older caddies were gentlemen. That is until they teed off. Once on the
fairways, some were not only terrible golfers, but temperamen-
tal. Caddying for a terrible golfer meant spending a lot of time
in the bushes looking for lost balls and sometimes lost clubs.

One Saturday morning, Dr. Armstrong checked in to
the caddy master, looking for a caddy. Since no other caddy
showed any interest, I volunteered. I soon discovered why the
opportunity had been declined by others. Dr. Armstrong had
one of the largest golf bags ever made. It was packed with
multiple collections of clubs. A heavy bag and a lousy golfer
are not a good combination for a caddy. Add to this his bad
temper and the doctor was a caddy's nightmare. On the 13th
green, he missed his putt. Enraged, he turned and hurled his
putter as far as he could and ordered me to retrieve it. I had
already retrieved a number of thrown clubs from prior holes.
That was it. I wasn't going to do it anymore. I told him my
job was to fetch his golf balls, not his golf clubs. He told me
to put his bag down and either get his putter or go back to the
clubhouse. I put his bag down, headed toward the clubhouse
and resigned my position as caddy. I never again returned to
the game, as a caddy, nor as a player. I think both the game
and I were better off.

During the summer break between my junior and senior
high school years, I asked Mr. Roy Seidel, the high school
"Dean of Boys" to provide me with a letter of recommendation for summer employment. With my recommendation in
hand, I went to the Libby, McNeil and Libby Cannery, which
was located on the north side of Chino Avenue, between 5th
and 6th streets. Some of the original structure is still standing.
I remember it was the season to can tomatoes. I went to the
employment office and knocked. A man's voice invited me in.
I entered and without looking up, the man asked, "Can I help
you?" I identified myself and handed him my letter of

recommendation. The man took one look at me, handed back the letter without opening it and said, "We're not hiring any more Mexicans." At the time, it felt so unfair, so undignified to be treated like that. Of course, in today's society, such treatment is not tolerated. To the cannery's credit, the following year I was hired to work during the orange season.

I also remember as a young child, around seven or eight years old, walking through downtown Chino and seeing signs in some of the business windows, "White Trade Only." I really didn't understand what that all meant, but I remember sensing that I wasn't welcome. By the time I was a teenager, those signs had been removed.

In 1940, many of Chino's young men joined the California National Guard. Their company's headquarters was the Pomona Armory. Since the National Guard only required certain weekend obligations, most recruits were able to retain their civilian jobs. One of these men was a 1939 Chino High graduate, Leo Fletcher. Leo was employed by the Chino Unified School District as a school bus driver. Soon after he joined the California National Guard, the United States Army assumed control under federalization and required full-time service from its members. Leo had to resign his position as a school bus driver. I applied for the open bus driver position. It was my senior year in high school. I was the only student applicant. Pearly Lowe, the Transportation Supervisor interviewed me. After passing the California Highway Patrol driving test, I was hired. Besides my regular driving duties, I drove my varsity baseball team and coach, Frank Elder, to our away games. This was the most responsible job I held as a teenager. I thought of it as a great privilege. I took it very seriously.

During the summer, between graduation from Chino High School in June of 1941 and my matriculation to Pomona Junior College (called today, Mount San Antonio College or Mt. SAC) in September, I decided to pick grapes in the Merced area

of the San Joaquin Valley. Many families living in the Chino
Barrio joined other families from southern California, migrating
to the San Joaquin Valley to take advantage of the grape and
cotton-picking seasons. Although my family didn't follow the
crops, I decided to go because many of my friends would be
gone for the summer. I stayed with the Gonzaleses (Paul and
Bob's family) in a migrant labor camp in the small community
of Planada, near Merced.

Working in the fields that summer was a milestone in
my young adulthood. It was an absolutely unforgettable learning experience. The way the growers and their foremen, who
were of mostly Mexican descent, treated the poorer and less-
educated farm workers was unconscionable. Too often, they
were demeaning, insulting, disgraceful and down right inhu-
mane. Cesar Chavez's successful endeavor to improve the
working conditions for the farm workers was, indeed, a remarkable and notable cause.

CHAPTER THREE

A CHINO MARINE IN THE SOUTH PACIFIC

A few months after I started my community college
career, the Imperial Forces of Japan struck Pearl Harbor. It
was December 7, 1941. I'll never forget that morning. It was a
Sunday and like most other Sunday mornings, I was playing
half-court basketball with some of my former high school
teammates. We played on the outside Chino High basketball
courts, located where the parking lot of the D.E.S. (Portuguese)
Hall is located today on Riverside Drive and 7th Street. Wes
Schulz, James Rappatoni, Sef Diaz, Roy Marabella, Leo Fletcher
and John Cummins were some of the guys playing that morning. After the game, we crossed Riverside Drive to the Chino
Malt Shop. It was on the south side of Riverside Drive and
across the alley from the First Methodist Church. We were sitting around the counter, sipping our cold drinks, cooling off,
when Bill Beck, a Chino High senior, burst through the doors
and shouted, "The Japanese are bombing Pearl Harbor!"

We had no idea what, where or who Pearl Harbor was,
but we did understand who the Japanese were and what bombing meant. What we didn't fully appreciate at the time was how
dramatically Pearl Harbor would affect our lives. Over the next
year, Wes Shulz joined the Navy. James Rappatoni became a
Navy Pilot. Sef Diaz joined the Marines and later received an

early medical discharge. Roy Marabella joined the Army Air Corps. Leo Fletcher was already an Army man and John Cummins joined the Marines.

John Esparza, another friend of ours and a Chino High graduate, became Chino's first casualty of WWII. John had joined the Army Air Corps prior to the war and was stationed in the Philippine Islands at the time the Japanese surprised us with their sneak attack on Pearl Harbor. He was first declared missing in action and later confirmed killed in action. John and his family lived just half a block from me. He was a bright young man hoping to become a United States citizen after his military service. He made his family and all of us proud.

I remained at Pomona Junior College long enough to be a starting athlete and earned letters in basketball and baseball. Shortly after Pearl Harbor was struck, the Pomona Junior College Basketball Team was returning from a scheduled game with Phoenix Junior College in Arizona. We were traveling in five cars. Somewhere between Beaumont and Redlands, all traffic heading west was stopped by the California Highway Patrol. The rumor quickly spread that enemy aircraft had been sighted over Los Angeles. On the western horizon we could faintly see the beams of the searchlights scanning the sky. By next morning, the news spread that the army was shooting at weather balloons launched from an enemy submarine. It's easy to understand the heightened nervousness of the time. In less than a year, I was marching in formation to the tune, "From the Halls of Montezuma."

Several months after Pearl Harbor, many of my male classmates at Pomona Junior College had either joined a select branch of the military or they had been drafted into the Army. I anticipated being drafted at any time. Under the circumstances it was difficult to focus on my studies. One evening I told my Dad I was going to quit school and go to work until I was called to duty. Dad, a strong advocate of education, simply replied, "Fine! Be ready to join me tomorrow morning."

Early the next morning, before daylight, he awakened me. "You'd better get ready. It's time to go." Half asleep, I hurried to get dressed and was told to grab the sack and clippers hanging on the outside wall. We grabbed our stuff, walked to the corner a block away and caught a ride in the back of a truck with other workers. We sat on hard wooden benches under a tarp rigged to cover the back like a covered wagon. We huddled together with our hands between our knees to stay warm. The older workers appeared most comfortable and talked as though they were in their own living rooms.

After what seemed like hours of traveling, the truck finally stopped and we all jumped out. We were surrounded by orange groves as far as we could see in the area that later became the city of Pico Rivera. I picked oranges alongside Dad. By midday, it was scorching hot and there was no breeze. In the middle of the groves, the heat was suffocating. I had worked in fields before as a laborer, but I always knew it was temporary. It was just for a summer or a week or two. This time, as days turned into weeks, I couldn't see any end. Every day we were faced with the same grueling task. After a couple of weeks, I told Dad I was going back to school. I remember him smiling and simply saying, "¡Que Bueno!"

Young men were required to register for the draft when they turned eighteen. My buddy, Marcie Morales, was three months older. He had received his orders to report for his physical and I had recently registered for the draft. He thought perhaps I would want to join the Army with him. I strongly suggested we join the U.S. Marine Corps instead. Prior to that time, I don't recall thinking about joining any particular branch of the armed services. However, I had had several conversations with two Chino Marines, Art Whittington and Reggie Martinez. Both were former Chino High School football players. They had enlisted in the Marines prior to December 7, 1941 and both were completely devoted to the Corps and its cause. They spoke in glowing terms of their pride in serving with the "Very Best." They claimed the Marines were "Number One," "Uncle Sam's Finest." "Semper Fidelis" ("Semper Fi" or "Always Faithful"), which I had never heard before, was Art and Reggie's most repeated slogan. Their other favorite slogan was, "Once a Marine, Always a Marine." Art was most convincing when he told me that if I wanted to be just another member of the Armed Forces, then I should join just any other branch of the military, but if I wanted to be the "Cream of the Crop" or the "Best of the Best" then the Marine Corps was the place for me.

Although I wasn't anywhere near as convincing as Art and Reggie, when I spoke to Marcie about joining the Marines, he agreed. One of my arguments was that if we were drafted into the Army, we could very well end up somewhere back East for our basic training, a long way from home. However, if we joined the Marines, there was only one location where we could be sent to boot camp training. It was the Marine Corps Recruit Depot located in San Diego, not too far from home. That was just what Marcie needed to hear to be convinced. We went and signed up with the United States Marines Corps.

Art Whittington became one of Chino's first casualties of World War II. He was lost over Wake Island in the Central Pacific Ocean in the early stages of the war. After faithful service, Reggie returned home and became a Veteran of Foreign Wars. Reggie died some years later. I never had the chance to ask them if they were unofficial recruiters for the Marine Corps.

Before we left for Marine Boot Camp, friends would warn us of the fierceness of the program. They said that Boot Camp knew no mercy and the discipline required was unyielding. They weren't exaggerating, but not one of our platoon succumbed to the intense and vigorous undertaking. I truly believe now that the program better prepared us for the realities of what we would be facing later on in the battlefield.

All too soon, on one cool summer morning in 1942, it was time to report. Marcie's uncle, Andy Morales, drove Marcie and me to the post office building in San Bernardino. Along with Andy were Marcie's dad and mom, Marcelino and Soledad Morales and Irene. I remember waving to them from the upstairs window as they drove away. It must have been tough on them. I know it was tough for Marcie and me.

We were joined with a dozen or more Marine volunteers and were given a mini physical before boarding a Greyhound bus for the Los Angeles main post office building. One very disappointed young man was sent home. He had failed the mini physical. In Los Angeles, we were joined with hundreds of others from all over southern California. We spent the rest of the day enduring extremely vigorous physical and mental examinations.

It was dark before those of us who prevailed were sworn in. Again, some were sent home. We were walked (we didn't know how to march the Marine Corps way, yet) to the Greyhound Bus Station on the corner of Fifth and Main Streets and loaded into buses headed to the Marine Recruit Depot in San Diego. Driving under blackout conditions, the buses kept their lights on low and traveled slowly. When we arrived around 4 a.m., a contemptuous, sneering and cussing sergeant, who wasn't too delighted to leave his sack (get out of bed), greeted us. His demeanor personified the tone of our entire Boot Camp experience.

Boot camp was the most structured and disciplined learning and conditioning environment I had ever experienced. Three months isn't very long to mold a bunch of soft civilians to the Corps' concept of what a Marine should be.

Marcie and I were assigned to Platoon 727. Our drill instructor (DI) was a career Marine named Sergeant Miller. Sergeant Miller had been aboard the Navy aircraft carrier, the USS Lexington, during the Battle of the Coral Sea. On May 8, 1942, the Lexington sunk into the depths of the ocean after a brutal Japanese onslaught. Sergeant Miller was one of the survivors. He had red hair and steely blue eyes. His military bearing was that of a Marine's Marine. His uniform always looked as if he had just stepped out of a recruiting poster. By the time he was finished with us, we looked and felt like proud United States Marines.

During our time in the Marine Recruit Depot, Sergeant Miller either made you or broke you. He had a way of getting inside your head. He first made you feel as if you were nothing worthless lowly civilians, barely worthy of his time or attention. If you ever wanted to truly become a Marine, you understood that you had to earn it and you earned it by doing everything the Drill Sergeant commanded you to do and you did it "on the double." If you made a mistake, you performed the task again and again until you got it right. Some days were absolutely g-r-u-e-l-i-n-g.

Sergeant Miller didn't seem to care whether or not we could even do what he commanded. It was our obligation to follow his orders, no matter what, and so we did. If any "boot" ever had the slightest urge to complain, Sergeant Miller implemented his attitude adjustment methods which were always effective. Nobody complained twice and most learned not to complain at all by watching what happened to those few who did.

Day in and day out of this kind of conditioning had a dramatic effect on me. I believe the change was for the better. I remember the few times Marcie and I were allowed to visit home before being shipped out. Our friends and family commented on how much we had changed in such a short period of time. We discovered later, in the heat of battle, how necessary these changes were for our survival and success. On the eve of the war with Iraq in 2003, Major General J. N. Mattis, USMC and Commanding General of the 1st Marine Division, addressed the Marines Corps in his, "Message to All Hands." The last line of his message captured well the obligation we felt as U.S. Marines, "Demonstrate to the world there is 'No Better Friend, No Worse Enemy' than a U.S. Marine. Semper Fidelis."

Sergeant Miller's Assistant Drill Instructor was Corporal Willhite. Although a strong disciplinarian, Corporal Willhite, not a career Marine, was an entirely different breed than Sergeant Miller. Sergeant Miller was polished and commanded a genuine respect. He was the Marine we all wanted to become.

For a couple of weeks during boot camp, we were transferred to the Linda Vista Rifle Range near San Diego. We were admonished in no uncertain terms by our pugnacious and burly Marine Sergeants that failure to qualify was not an option. We were taught to hit targets hundreds of yards away from various positions in varying wind conditions. There were three categories for qualification: Marksman, Sharp Shooter and Expert. I qualified as a Sharp Shooter.

Many of the boot camp graduation requirements considered indispensable by the Corps never made much sense to me. But I confess that I enjoyed the obstacle courses. Deep inside, I always wanted to be first at whatever I did, especially shooting at the rifle range on qualifying day. I never finished first, but came close on several occasions. In striving to be first, I always thought I did better than I would have done otherwise.

Our first issue of gear, which included our greens (uniforms), was handed out, regardless of our size. One can imagine what we looked like in our one-size fits all uniforms. Sergeant Miller was right. We looked like a bunch of "sad sacks." However, ten days or so before graduation, after our body fat was nearly all burned away, we were taken to the boot camp tailor shop and our uniforms were fitted for graduation. We were finally given our Marine Corps emblems to compliment our newly fitted uniforms. We smartly paraded before the Commanding General while the band played the Marine Corps Hymn. We were the result of Sergeant Miller's herculean effort to mold us from "sad sacks" to U.S. Marines. He would eventually and relunctantly admit that we had made the grade.

In hindsight, I recognize that the Marine Corps relied heavily on developing a strong sense of personal pride and responsibility within each Marine. It discouraged its members from feeling sorry for themselves. Once we graduated from boot camp, as Marines, we were always kept busy. Even when we were granted free time ("liberty"), we were required to present ourselves for inspection to assure that our appearance appropriately represented the Marine Corps. There were no allowances for a Marine to disrespect the pride of the Marine Corps.

Shortly after graduation, we were trucked to Camp Elliot, just north of San Diego, where we endured more intense training. Gratefully, we were allotted time to visit home a few times before we were finally shipped out to be the Marines we were trained to be. Despite our extensive training, we remained apprehensive of the challenges ahead.

It was a cool evening when we pulled out of San Diego Harbor and headed west. Besides Marcie and I, there were two other Chino Marines on board that troop ship. I wasn't aware that Paul Gonzales and Tony Partida from Chino had joined the Marines and that we were all on board. It was a pleasant surprise to find them there. Paul had been the star catcher on our Chino High School Baseball Team and Tony had lived half a block from me in the Chino Barrio.

I recall all four of us standing by the rail of the ship as the silhouette of lower California faded into the darkness of the evening, wondering to ourselves if and when we would ever come back home. We were assigned to different detachments and our living quarters were on different levels of the ship. I don't remember seeing any of my friends again while we were in transit.

Thirty-two days after leaving San Diego, seeing only the Pacific Ocean, we entered the New Caledonia Harbor in the South Pacific. New Caledonia became an essential Allied base during WWII. American troops occupied the Island in 1942 when it was threatened by the Japanese. The Island's capital, Noumea, was one of the U.S. Navy's principal anchorages in the South Pacific during WWII.

It was a huge morale booster to witness a large portion of the Allied Military Might concentrated in one harbor. It made us feel much less vulnerable, despite our long distance from home. After the month long journey, we were all weary of the crowded, sticky and smelly ship. It was hard to believe that our home at sea had once been the luxurious Hawaiian cruise ship, the Lurline. World War II called for an all-out effort from freedom loving nations to halt the tyranny plaguing the world and to develop the level of liberty and democracy necessary for a better existence. The conversion of our nation's luxury cruise ships was just a small material part of the overall sacrifice. The real sacrifice would be made by over 400,000 Americans who would give up their lives and tens of thousands more who would suffer from life-long injuries and disabilities for the cause of freedom in WWII. Of course, we weren't alone. Millions of people from other nations would also suffer and perish for the cause. In the end, it would take an unprecedented giving of life to depose an unprecedented demonstration of tyranny. I hate to consider where we would be today without our nation's willingness to sacrifice.

Since we were the first Marine replacement battalion of the Pacific War, we were deployed in many different directions

from New Caledonia. I didn't have the chance to locate any of
my Chino friends and I didn't have any idea to where they had
been transferred. Eventually, I learned that Marcie had gone to
a Special Weapons Battalion attached to the First Marine
Division and Tony had ended up with the 17th Marines of the
First Marine Division. Paul had joined a Marine Air Wing on
Guadalcanal. I was also assigned to Guadalcanal, where I
joined the First Marine Division and the "mop-up" operations
of that campaign. I didn't see Paul or Tony until we returned
home to Chino. The First Marine Division was moved from
Guadalcanal after the island, once secured, was turned over to
the Army. Some of us went to Australia and others to New
Zealand. I ended up in Ballarat, Australia for what is now
referred to as R and R (Rest and Recreation). There I was
assigned as a Forward Observer with Charlie Battery, 11th
Marines, First Marine Division. I later learned that Marcie was
also stationed in Ballarat. Although our outfits were physically
located at extreme ends of the Botanic Gardens where we were
quartered, we went on liberty together to downtown Ballarat as
often as possible. We always enjoyed sharing whatever news we
had from our families and friends in Chino. It was our way of
staying grounded.

Australia was the home of the First Marine Division
from January to August of 1943. The Australians were very
pleasant and friendly. They went out of their way to make us
feel at home. Perhaps they understood that if the Marines had
lost the Battle of Guadalcanal, Australia would have been within striking distance of the Japanese. Some of the Marines
developed strong relationships with the Aussies. Some married
Australian girls and returned there after the war.

For some Marines, it was difficult when the time came
for us to leave Australia. It meant they had to leave behind
newly acquired family and friends. But in early August of 1943,
the command or the "Close Station March Order" (CSMO) was

given. It was time to move out.

During the World's Fair in Brisbane in 1988, while I was a California State Senator, Irene and I visited Ballarat. I was impressed by the growth of the city since 1943. I spent some time with a young editor from the local newspaper. He took a photo of us standing in front of the cannon at the entrance to the Botanical Gardens. The cannon was a monument honoring the U.S. Marines once stationed there. The older Australians stilled refereed to us as "Yanks" and were most grateful for our participation in the defense of their country.

A few weeks after we returned home, I received a letter from a man in Hollywood, enclosing the article about my visit to Ballarat and the photo. Later, we talked on the phone. He told me he was a little boy in a Ballarat orphanage when I was based there. He pleasantly recalled the American Marines visiting the orphanage and giving the kids candy. He was now a successful chef at one of the major hotels in Hollywood. He kept in touch with his hometown by subscribing to the Ballarat News. He was grateful for our service. He also seemed excited to be speaking with someone who had lived in his hometown.

Following our orders, we were trucked some 50 miles from Ballarat to Melbourne, where we spent the night on the grandstands of the Melbourne Cricket Grounds with nothing but our GI ponchos for cover. I recall the strong, cold and penetrating wind bellowing through us throughout the night. I can't remember spending a night in colder weather. It was truly "bitter cold." The same cricket grounds were later demolished and reconstructed for the 1956 Olympics.

The next morning, we boarded our transports headed to the South Pacific Islands, still held by the Japanese. It was dark when we pulled out of the Melbourne Harbor. Many bonfires could be seen on the beach, lit by friends of the U.S. Marines who had gathered to bid us farewell. Early the next morning, the Australian Coast was but a memory.

It took a few days to reach our new destination. The sticky and smelly troop ship was all too familiar. As was always the case whenever we were in transit, we were never short on scuttlebutt (rumors) as to where we were headed next. Our destination this time was Buna on the Island of New Guinea.

New Guinea is hot and humid. Most of the island is a thick rainforest full of rich wildlife. It's the second largest island in the world. Mostly mountainous, the Owen Stanley Mountain range dominates the terrain. Among the coastal low-lands, lies one of the largest swamps in the world. Melanesians make up the majority of the population in New Guinea.

With new replacements arriving everyday, we were finally told that the First Marine Division was up to its full fighting capacity. It turned out that one of the replacements was Jess Ontiveros from Pomona. Jess was an outstanding football player when he attended Pomona High School and I attended Pomona Jr. College. We visited just once. Regrettably, Jess was killed in action a few days later. After I returned to the States, while waiting for a bus in Los Angeles, his mother and sister approached me. They wanted to know all I knew about Jess. They told me that in his last letter he mentioned running into me and going over old times. I shared with them what I could remember about our conversation. I told them of my great fondness and respect for Jess. They appreciated hearing from one of his friends, despite the painfulness of the circumstance.

In New Guinea, we were regularly bombed and strafed by enemy aircraft, not to mention our continual exposure to enemy sniper fire. Despite the dangerous distractions, the Division's focus was getting prepared for our next campaign. We knew our next landing was inevitable. Relief maps of the Island of New Britain in the Bismarck Archipelago were studied frequently. New Britain had an airstrip at Rabaul, which the Japanese effectively used to monitor and observe American Military traffic in the region. General Douglas MacArthur, the supreme commander of the Allied Forces in the Pacific, wanted the Marines to remove the menacing obstacle.

I vividly remember seeing the massive throng of combat Marines, with their war paraphernalia on Oro Bay, as we boarded a Tank Landing Ship (LST) headed for war. Among the flurry of men and equipment, we felt a profound sense of camaraderie as we swarmed from the beach and boarded the LSTs, which were positioned for easy access. We boarded through the LST's massive front gate. When lowered, it converted into a loading ramp. Our LST was already loaded with our equipment, including artillery howitzers and tanks.

Once we were situated inside, the huge gate gradually raised up until it finally clanged shut. After a short delay, the "All clear" sounded and the engines started. Rough vibrations shook the ship as it struggled to pull away from the beach. We were leaving New Guinea for what turned out to be an overnight journey across the Huron Gulf to the enemy-held island of New Britain. This was the area where Navy Lieutenant Jack Kennedy, in his PT 109, was rammed by a Japanese destroyer on the night of August 2, 1943.

It was night as we sailed to New Britain Island. I remember that except for the steady murmur of the engines, an eerie quiet prevailed. Conversation was minimal. Some of the men cleaned their weapons over and over again, each consumed by his own thoughts. Warrant Officer Sack, a career Marine, tried to break the tension by shouting, "Damn Japs kept us awake at night. Now we're going to give' em an early reveille." A few responded with quiet smurks.

Once on our way, we were allowed to go top deck to get some fresh air. It was a cloudy night, with the moon's light breaking through the cover on occasion. Several times we could see silhouetted islands against the horizon, as we passed by. The feeling was surreal.

The command finally came, "All hands return to your

units!" Back below, we were given our last explicit orders on
what was expected once we hit the beach. The Marines'
Chaplain led us in prayer and we were "at the ready." We could
hear aircraft overhead and hoped they were ours. Nearby bat-
tleships began to shell the island. We could hear the projectiles
pass overhead, sounding like runaway trains sucking the air
behind them, screaming to their targets. Then we heard explosions in the distance as our air cover (our own 5th Air Force)
descended upon the enemy held beach, strafing and bombard-
ing the Japanese. Finally, the engines of the LST began to slow
down and we felt the ship's hull grind against the sandy beach.
The explosions grew louder and more frequent. Over the
ship's speakers, we heard, "Marines, this is no drill - Prepare to
disembark ... Good Luck!." The LST's huge front gate began
to lower slowly.

We were all "at the ready" on one knee when the
opened gate finally hit the sand. Like horses out of the gate,
we poured out of our protective cocoon, onto the naked beach.
Many of us scrambled for cover toward the tangled mass of
jungle ahead of us. Others rushed to unload the heavy equipment from the LST. This was it - a specific point in time when
fear and discipline joined together to face the enemy. Duly
indoctrinated that we had to prevail, failure was not an option.

We were told that our Navy and Army Air Corps were
completing their missions, minimizing the enemy's strength and
position on the beach. Back home it was Christmas morning.
For us it was the 26th of December 1943. At 0748 we stormed
the beach at Cape Gloucester on the Island of New Britain.
Our initial objective was to take control of the beach and move
inland as quickly as possible. After relatively light resistance, we
accomplished our initial mission. The beach was secured.

Unfortunately, we suffered severe casualties from
"friendly fire" from our own "air cover" as the First Marine

Division advanced to secure the airstrip. We were also met with fanatical opposition from the Japanese Imperial Marines.

Suffering our share of casualties, the airstrip was ultimately taken. The miserable weather was a form of opposition few of us had experienced before. Within a few months of our landing, New Britain Island was under our complete control.

New Britain is an island about 300 miles long and 50 miles wide. The island has many rivers, swamps and thick tropical rain forests. Some jungle areas are nearly impenetrable. It rained heavily during most of our operations. The rains would stop occasionally, leaving the hot tropical sun to beat down upon us. It was extremely humid, muggy and uncomfortable. When the sun came out, our clothes, drenched from the previous rain, would dry within minutes, leaving a sticky residue.

It's important to note that the First Marine Replacement Battalion's first casualty didn't occur in the heat of battle at Guadacanal, New Guinea, or New Britain. It occurred at our dispatch point at New Caledonia. We had to climb down a rope landing net slung over the side of the transport ship to the much smaller landing boat below. The landing boat would lunge up and down, six to twelve feet, every time a wave hit the side of the transport ship. We watched in horror as one of our buddies lost his grip on the rope landing net and plunged into merciless ocean waters. He disappeared between the transport ship and the landing boat. He didn't have a chance with all the gear loaded on his back. He was our first casualty.

After securing the beach on Cape Gloucester, as Forward Observers, we were sent on a reconnaissance mission farther inland. Approaching a river, Captain Moyer requested and was provided an intelligence report indicating there was no evidence of enemy presence on the opposite bank. The river was 3 to 4 yards deep and about 125 yards wide. We needed to cross it. We inflated a rubber raft and eight men boarded. The current was strong and we struggled to paddle across the river.

"Up From Second Street"   Ruben S. Ayala

We were headed for a clearing on the opposite bank when about halfway across the river, we were bombarded with enemy rifle and mortar fire. Our cover, positioned on our side of the river, immediately responded with counter fire. We were in the middle of a firefight. Ammunition was flying all around us. During the heated exchange, our raft was hit and sunk almost instantly. We lost one of our buddies from a direct hit. It all happened so fast.

With our packs and added equipment dangling from our backs and our steel helmets and "ammo" belts still in place, we immediately sank to the bottom of the river. Under water, we desperately struggled to remove our gear. I don't have the foggiest idea how long we were on the bottom of that river. I remember trying to push myself up with all my strength to the water's surface. The weight of my gear was just too much. I remember I had just removed my helmet and "ammo" belt when I was grabbed by my hair and pulled to the surface. Gasping for air and choking, I was pulled towards the shore. Luckily, the current carried us down stream away from enemy fire. Dazed and confused, we finally dragged ourselves onto the friendly shore. In the chaos, one of us didn't make it. Most of us were apparently in a state of shock. I faintly recall lying on my back as a Navy Corpsman (medic) straddled over me. He broke a pencil-size glass ampoule in half and removed a needle and gave me an injection. I later learned he had inject-ed me with morphine. Almost immediately, I experienced an indescribable euphoria, lasting throughout the night. I was told I slept through an air raid and incoming fire.

As a result of my only experience with morphine, I can honestly say that I fully understand how many veterans later struggled with addiction to morphine after being exposed to it on the battlefield. Those with lasting injuries and resulting chronic pain were the most vulnerable. World-boxing champi-on, Barney Ross, was one of them. After a heroic 13-hour standoff defending a foxhole against the Japanese at Guadalcanal, Barney Ross was left with painful shrapnel injuries to his legs and sides. After many difficult years struggling with morphine, Barney ultimately overcame his addiction.

A few days later I learned that my Marine buddy who had pulled me to the river's surface, saving my life, was young "Chick" Williamson from Alabama. He was known as "Chick" because he claimed to be only sixteen years old. Some of us believed he was even younger since "Chick" didn't have to shave to stand inspections. A couple of years later we ran into each other while stationed at the Marine Rest Camp in Klamath Falls, Oregon. It was great to see "Chick" again and thank him once more for saving my life. We had the chance to sit down for dinner under much more pleasant surroundings. I've often considered all that I would have missed in life had "Chick" not been there at that critical moment. Thanks again, "Chick!"

Paul Gonzales, my long-time hometown buddy, also served at Guadacanal. He told me years later of his experience on a rescue mission off the Coast of Guadacanal. The U.S. Navy had been hit and damaged by enemy aircraft the night before. Navy personnel had been floating in the ocean in their life jackets all night long. Paul's detachment was there the next morning in small boats rescuing the men from the water. After assisting two survivors, Paul reached down to help another sailor. When the sailor turned his face towards Paul, Paul could barely believe his eyes. Could it really be? It was. The sailor was Harry Nichols, a Chino High classmate of ours. Halfway around the world, one friend, a Chino Marine, was rescuing another friend, a Chino Navy man, out of the waters of the South Pacific. For these two men, a very large and tumultuous world rather quickly became a very small and comforting one. Paul recently passed away on December 27, 2003.

I don't remember seeing any of my Chino friends while in New Guinea. I didn't know if any of them would take part in the Cape Gloucester Campaign. I found out after the campaign began that Marcie was on board one of the other LSTs and had gone ashore some 150 yards from my unit during the beach landing. Two days later, as my column was moving inland, I ran into a boot camp buddy named Moody. He told me that Marcie's Special Weapons Unit had been hit heavily by sniper fire. Marcie had been killed. I went numb. I'll never forget that day. It was Marcie's 21st birthday.

A week later, back at our bivouac area (temporary encampment), I approached Captain Fitzgerald, the on-duty officer, and requested permission to walk to the makeshift cemetery. It was a few miles toward the beach. I told him I had lost a buddy from home and that we had joined the Marines together. I wanted to find him. Sympathetically, he turned my request down, reminding me that other men in our unit could make the same request and he couldn't afford to let us all go. The area between our encampment and the cemetery was not yet totally secure and he didn't want us rambling through the jungle unless we were under official orders.

I walked away disappointed. I was determined to locate Marcie's grave. I sloshed my way through the dense jungle, towards the cemetery. In retrospect, I could have been in deep trouble. Directly disregarding an order in the field is an extremely serious violation. But at the time, all I was thinking was that I had to find my best friend.

I was soaked when I reached the makeshift cemetery. The shallow graves were lined up in short rows. Wooden crosses held the dog tags marking each grave. The newest graves had only palm branches with dog tags lying on top as markers. I was looking for Marcie's dog tags when the cemetery's custodian spotted me. He asked me who I was looking for. I told him. He knew both Marcie and me from Camp Elliot.

"Oh, Morales isn't here. He was airlifted out this morning," he said. "He may lose an arm, but he'll be all right." I stood there in shock. I couldn't believe it. Marcie was alive and he was going to be okay. This was a dramatic turn. I was overwhelmed. I don't recall how I found my way back to my unit.

I wouldn't meet up with Marcie until Irene's graduation from Chaffey College in June of 1944. You can only imagine what it was like to see each other after so long and after so much. In the meantime, just knowing he was okay was enough for me.

The Cape Gloucester Campaign was typical of other Marine Corps actions in the Pacific during World War II. The Imperial Forces of Japan were willing to die for their emperor. Many would not yield, nor would they be taken alive as prisoners. With their fanatical mentality, the Japanese were a fierce, dreaded and formidable enemy. But with unflinching fortitude, the Allied Forces, including the U.S. Marines, would not consent to the Japanese Empire's diabolical designs. Time and time again, we would prove ourselves victorious.

George McMillan, the author of the <u>THE OLD BREED - A History of the First Marine Division in World War II</u>, described the added struggle of the natural environment well. He wrote:

"The fighting man expects that his vocation will carry him to unlikely and alien places. That is all right. It is one of the things he may look forward to. But there is a degree of strangeness beyond the bounds of the bargain, the bargain being: the natural hazards of the battlefield must never equal the hazards contrived by the enemy.

"Break this law, put a fighting man down in a spot where the plant and animal life and the climate are as much or more of a menace to his existence than the armed human opposite him, and the fighting man will feel he is the victim of an injustice.

"That is why the men who fought at Cape Gloucester remember the place more for the jungle than for the Japanese."

(Chapter 14, Par.1, page 175, Infantry Journal Press, 1949)

As described by Marine historians, "...the 1st Marine Division was a battle tested, veteran organization that had the distinction of leading America's first offensive of World War II on Guadalcanal in August 1942. Emerging victorious after the epic six month campaign, the Old Breed stopped Japan's threatened advance toward Australia. In December 1943, the Division was called upon again to attack the Cape Gloucester area of western New Britain. The Marines' eventual victory there ensured the encirclement and neutralization of Japan's fortress at Rabaul, and opened the door to General MacArthur's move to retake the Philippines."
(www.pelelu.net/USForces/1stmardv.htm)

During our tour of duty in the Pacific, many Marines came down with all kinds of tropical diseases. I was no exception. My acute symptoms were high fever, lack of appetite and abnormal weight loss (50 pounds). The Marines with the more severe cases were returned to the States as soon as replacements became available. I was one of them. I was taken to an Army hospital at Port Moresby, New Guinea and then transferred to the Naval Hospital in Brisbane, Australia. From there I returned to the States and was hospitalized at the Oak Knoll Hospital in Oakland, California.

Once stateside, my itinerary took me from the Oak Knoll Hospital to the San Diego Recruit Depot, then to Camp Lejeune, North Carolina. There were four of us on the train to Camp Lejeune. Curiously, we weren't allowed to enter certain train cars. The train stopped at a small town in the middle of the New Mexico desert. Through our window we could see men in uniform exiting from the train cars that we weren't allowed to enter. Guarded by Army Military Police, the men lined up single-file on the station platform. The American Red Cross provided hot coffee and donuts to the men while we watched from the train. They were prisoners of war.

Despite our U.S. Military uniforms, we weren't extended the same courtesy.

From Camp Lejeune, I ended up at the Naval hospital located in Portsmouth, Virginia. It was there where I made two profound decisions, laying the groundwork for the rest of my life. I called Irene at her California Hospital Nurses' Residence (Room 411) in Los Angeles and asked her to marry me. I don't remember how long it took her to respond, but she said, "Yes!"

The other important decision was to register to vote. This was my first time. Not knowing nor caring about the differences between Democrats and Republicans, I didn't have a ready answer when I was asked what party I wanted to join. I remembered the Presidential race was going on. President Roosevelt had made the argument that since we were in the middle of a world war, it wasn't a good idea to "change horses in the middle of stream." I agreed and registered as a Democrat. I've been a Democrat ever since, although I haven't always agreed with the Democratic Platform or voted along Party lines. In many ways, I feel like the Democratic Party has steadily drifted away from what it first represented to me. I've always tried to evaluate each issue on its own merits and vote according to common sense and good conscience despite either party's position. To this day, I don't believe that Democrats nor Republicans hold an exclusive on having the right answers.

While a patient at the Naval hospital at Norfolk, Virginia, Navy doctors gave me permission to travel to New York and attend the U.S. Army West Point Academy versus the University of Notre Dame Football game. It was my first experience traveling on the East Coast. From my Pullman porthole, the scenery was breathtaking as we traveled north from Chesapeake Bay through Washington D.C. to Philadelphia and on to New York. It was a beautifully cold autumn afternoon.

When I finally arrived at the Polo Grounds, football fans were already gathering outside the stadium. The Army team bus had just arrived. As the players exited the buses, I was able to get the attention of Army's All-American Glen Davis. We had played against each other when Glen was attending Bonita High School in LaVerne and I was at Chino High. The Army/Notre Dame game was sold out and Glen asked whether I had a ticket. I didn't. We shook hands and I wished him good luck. As he left to join his teammates, he said something about going to see what he could do. A few minuted later, a young man appeared and handed a ticket to me and to a sailor who happened to be standing next to me. The tickets were for box seats right next to Frank Sinatra and Sportscaster Bill Stern. Army had little trouble defeating Notre Dame that Saturday. What a game! I still have the game program autographed by both celebrities.

From Virginia, I was transferred across the country to a Marine rest camp in the middle of the Klamath Mountains in Oregon. To my delight, the camp commander was Medal of Honor recipient Captain Joe Foss. The company commander was Captain Mitchell Paige, also a Medal of Honor winner. Captain Foss, a Marine fighter pilot, earned his medal for his record twenty-six aerial victories over Guadalcanal. Captain Paige earned his for his undeniable courage as a platoon sergeant during the ground battle for Guadalcanal.

Klamath Falls was a wartime rehabilitation center for returning Marines from the Pacific who suffered reoccurring symptoms from tropical diseases. Most of us had a history of malaria. The objective was to return the men to active duty as soon as possible. The typical stay was about three months. At the end of their time, with the Navy doctor's approval, the men were given a ten-day tolerance test to test their endurance. We were warned, "If you don't pass the tolerance test, you're going to wish to hell you had." The camp was located about five miles from the City of Klamath Falls, where we went on liberty and sometimes walked back to camp in the snow.

At Klamath Falls, I ran into fellow Chinoan Elmer "Dobie" Gray. Dobie had joined the Marines in the late 1930's. He came from a Chino pioneer family. The old Gray residence is now a historical building, located across the street from the 7th Street Community Theatre. It currently houses the Chino Valley Chamber of Commerce. When Dobie's younger brother, Bob, left the Chino City Council, I was elected to fill that seat. Bob Gray later bought my insurance agency.

Passing the tolerance test, we were given the choice of our next duty station. San Pedro was the closest Marine facility to Chino. The Naval disciplinary barracks was located on Terminal Island, sandwiched between San Pedro and Long Beach. The USNDB housed around 2,500 Sailors, Marines, Coast Guards and Seabees who had been court-martialed for felonious activities. Their violations ranged from "going over the hill" (Absent without leave or AWOL) to murder.

In command of the barracks was Navy Captain Jack Kennedy, a tough career mustang. Mustangs were what the Navy called officers who started as enlisted men and worked their way up through the ranks to become officers. They were considered the backbone of the Navy. Major Ball was the Commander of the Marine detachment in charge of security. There were no ACLU representatives, no friends on the outside, nor any coddling going on at this command. Captain Kennedy frequently reminded the inmates that he had no use for them. They were a disgrace to their nation. He reminded them that while their buddies were at war getting shot, they were nice and safe because they had gotten their noses dirty. They were warned not to break any of his rules. "If you do, don't get caught" was his most frequent saying.

I arrived on a Saturday afternoon. The next day, I wandered around getting acquainted with my new environment. By Sunday afternoon, my name appeared on the next morning's duty roster. On Monday morning, armed with a weapon and an MP armband, I went on duty. As I stepped off the van to replace the Marine Sentry, the Sergeant of the Guard bellowed at me, "Don't turn your back on these S.O.B.s and don't screw up." That was the beginning and the end of my official training. It hardly compared to the extensive academy training that California Correctional Officers receive today, but the Sergeant made his point.

The U.S. Navy disciplinary barracks presented me with a different kind of challenge. I didn't get any satisfaction from being in command of hundreds of malcontents. While in charge of the Sally Port Gate, it was my responsibility to make sure all inmates returned from their work details. The upside, however, was that I was now stationed a short distance from Los Angeles where Irene was pursuing her academic and professional aspirations at the California Hospital School of Nursing and USC. I hitchhiked almost weekly up and down Figueroa Street from San Pedro to Los Angeles. Since I didn't own a car, we did a lot of walking and patronized the Street Car System, mostly the J or P street cars.

To complete her communicable disease work for her nursing degree, Irene had to go San Francisco, to the San Francisco City Hospital for about two months. When she returned to Los Angeles, we set the date for our wedding.

July 22, 1945 was our very special day. We went shopping for our rings in downtown Los Angeles, buying them from Leroy Jewelers on Broadway. They allowed us to finance the purchase, issuing me my first credit card.

The wedding was held in Irene's hometown church, Our Lady of Guadalupe Catholic Church. It was and still is located about a block from where I was born and two blocks from where Irene grew up. It was your typical wartime wedding, but well attended by many friends and relatives. Marcie was my best man. He had received an honorable medical discharge from the Marines, but was still nursing wounds to his right arm and midsection. He donned his Marine Corps "Greens" one more time for our very special day. Marcie lived in Chino with his wife, Genevieve (Deenie), and their sons, just three blocks from the Ayalas, until he passed away on April 18, 2003. Their three sons are: Jim-an assistant physical therapist, Pat-an engineer and Bill-an attorney. Deenie's brother, Jay Rodriguez, was my campaign manager when I ran for San Bernardino County Supervisor in 1966.

Irene's younger sister, Mary, was Irene's maid of honor. Mary lives in Chino with her husband, George Encinas, and their family. Connie, Irene's older sister, was also a great help with the wedding. She stayed in Los Angeles with us when our son, Bud, was born. Connie also lives in Chino. Her husband, Richard Salgado, passed away on September 8, 2004.

After our vows were exchanged and I kissed my beautiful bride, the older folks gathered at Irene's parent's home for the reception. The younger crowd carried the reception to the American Legion Hall, now the Chino Community building. After the festivities, Richard Mogle, my father's employer, with his wife Alma, drove us to the Mission Inn in Riverside for our honeymoon. The Mission Inn was originally built in 1876 and is a historic landmark in Riverside, California, occupying an entire city block. Several U.S. Presidents have visited the Mission Inn over the last few decades, most recently, President George W. Bush. At the time and to this day, the Mission Inn is a favorite wedding spot and honeymoon destination.

Two days later they picked us up. It was their wedding gift to us. We were most grateful, especially since we still didn't own a car and gasoline was rationed. To this day, we hold a special spot in our hearts for the Mission Inn.

Irene's friends from the hospital stayed for the reception and then returned to Los Angeles. Some had to go on duty. A day after our honeymoon, Irene was back at the Nurses' Residence and I returned to the Marine Barracks.

We continued to see each other as often as possible, mostly on weekends.

It wasn't long before my name, along with other members of the detachment, appeared on the bulletin board as eligible for deployment. Scuttlebutt (rumor mill) was at its best. Rumors ranged from us being transferred to Camp Pendleton near Oceanside, to being deployed to a full-scale invasion of the Japanese Mainland. In the midst of our growing anxiety, on August 6, 1945, the U.S. dropped the first atomic bomb on the Japanese City of Hiroshima, devastating it. The demand by U.S. led Allied forces for an unconditional surrender was ignored. The Japanese Government sat on its hands and did nothing. President Harry Truman ultimately authorized the second atomic bomb to be dropped three days later on August 9th. Nagasaki was the target.

Japan finally surrendered unconditionally. On August 15th, Emperor Hirohito declared to the Japanese people that Japan had lost the war. On September 2, 1945, the Japanese, under the direction of Army General Douglas MacArthur, signed the formal surrender aboard the Battleship USS Missouri, anchored at Tokyo Bay.

President Truman has been severely criticized by some as acquiescing to his military advisors in authorizing the use of such a devastating device. While it is unquestionably true that many civilians were casualties of the atomic bomb, abruptly ending the war saved countless more American and Japanese lives. One insider, who had struggled beforehand with the potential consequences of actually dropping the atomic bomb, later commented, "There is one point that was missed … that was the effect the bomb would have in so shocking the Japanese that they could surrender without losing face … we didn't realize its value to give the Japanese such a shock that they could surrender without complete loss of face." (David E. Lilienthal, The Journals of David E. Lilienthal, Volume Two:

The Atomic Energy Years, 1945-1950, page 198).

    The worst of tyranny was deposed for the time. The United Nations was soon established. The Marshall Plan followed. Seeds of democracy were planted and gradually took root in Japan and Germany. An unprecedented, yet often fractured, era of prosperity and peace for the entire world has been the result. Our challenge today is to incorporate the hard earned lessons and sacrifices of yesteryear. We must continue to subdue the forces of terror while developing a world community founded upon proven principles of individual freedom and responsibility in order to provide a sustainable prosperity for all.

"Up From Second Street"   Ruben S. Ayala

CHAPTER FOUR

A NEW BEGINNING

With the war successfully ending and the immense joy that followed somewhat subsiding, men and women in uniform began to return to their loved ones and experience civilian life once again. The system devised to muster out those with reserve status allotted credit for the number of months of active duty and the number of months of actual combat experience. Those with the highest number of credits were discharged first. Marcie and I had voluntarily joined the regular Marine Corps, so we didn't have any reserve status. I had to serve out the time left of my four-year enlistment. I was finally given an honorable discharge from the Marine Corps in August of 1946.

Sometime after my return to the States, I received a letter from a long-time Chino friend, Rudy Martinez. Rudy was a few years younger than I and had also become a U.S. Marine. Although there were five Marine Divisions in the Pacific Theatre during WWII, Rudy was assigned to my old overseas outfit, the 11th Marines of the First Marine Division. Our paths never crossed during the war. It turns out that Rudy ended up fighting in the battles of Peleliu and Okinawa, both vicious fights against a fanatical enemy. In both cases, the U.S. prevailed, but only after suffering tremendous loss of life. I was greatly relieved to hear that Rudy had returned home safely.

Rudy's father, Manuel, was a great friend, too. On

Sundays, he often played baseball with us. Despite being older than the rest of us, Rudy's father was an outstanding baseball player. After the war, Manuel started up a private bus service, running between Chino and Pomona. Years later, during my first year as a County Supervisor, I was involved in a serious automobile accident. After some time in the hospital, I was required to follow a strict regimen for rehabilitation, which included daily long walks. On one such walk along Riverside Drive, Manuel was returning from his stop in Pomona with a busload of passengers. Seeing me walking along the side of the road, he stopped the bus and offered me a ride. The passengers joined in, urging me to get on board. I felt like a celebrity. I had to explain my motivations for walking and respectfully decline, but I was grateful for the reminder of our lasting friendship.

By the time I returned to civilian ranks, many of my peers with reserve status had a head start on me due to their earlier discharges. One of the first things I did was to purchase, with part of my mustering-out pay, a 1936 Chevrolet four-door sedan from a friend. It was blue with yellow wheels and it was all mine.

In 1947, Irene graduated from the California Hospital School of Nursing, affiliated with the University of Southern California (USC). She was employed at the California Hospital in Los Angeles after serving as a member of the United States Cadet Nurse Corps. My desire was to major in electrical engineering. I wanted to attend USC under the GI bill, but due to the discharge system, I had a late start and fellow veterans had already filled the eligible slots for the year. I would have to wait, but waiting around isn't what I do best. Instead, I went over to Figueroa and Santa Barbara Streets and was admitted to the National School for Radio and Television. Under the GI Bill, the government paid my tuition, plus $90 a month for subsistence. I graduated in 1948.

As a school project, I built, from a telekit, one of the first television sets in Chino. Irene's folks paid the cost. Many old-timers still remember going over to the Morales' home to watch what was then a remarkable new invention. It was a black and white television with a ten-inch screen.

I was still attending school when we rented our first home. It was a ground-floor apartment of a large two-story home that had been converted into several apartments, located at 963 South Hoover in West Los Angeles. It had a large living room that doulbled as a bedroom, a tiny kitchen and a three-quarter bathroom. We stored a rollaway bed in the living room closet during the day and brought it out to sleep on at night. As part of the rent, I agreed to mow the front lawn, sweep the stairway and take the garbage containers to the front curb for pickup. It was a comfortable setting and a good beginning.

It wasn't long before we were sharing the rented home with our two sons, Bud and Eddie. Ruben Marcie (Bud) was born at the California Hospital on November 2, 1947. Bud was a strong and husky baby with curly brown hair. He was easygoing and usually slept through the night. Maurice Edward (Eddie) was also born at the California Hospital. He was born on April 6, 1949. Eddie was healthy, alert and a handful. He was curious about everything. He kept us awake on many a night.

Andy Morales Jr. and Oscar Lopez helped us move from our Los Angeles apartment, which we had outgrown, to Pomona, for a while, and then back to our roots and family. We rented a house on Chino Avenue. Gary Randall, our third son, arrived soon after. He was born at the Pomona Community Hospital on July 7, 1952. A sweet and healthy baby, his older brothers took a keen interest in their new baby brother. They looked after him very closely.

Before Gary was born, Irene and I received approval for a Cal-Vet loan to start building our own house in Chino.

"Up From Second Street"   Ruben S. Ayala

We purchased a lot and a half on Rhodes Place and Clyde Mitchell, a Chino High School classmate, drew up the plans for us. When I brought Irene and Gary home from the hospital after Gary's birth, we stopped to see the wooden framework under construction. It was an exciting time. We monitored the construction progress weekly and a few months later in 1952, we moved into our new home in Chino.

Upon graduation from the National School for Radio and Television, I went to work for the Admiral Television Corporation of Chicago, Illinois, as a field representative working out of Los Angeles. In the fall of 1950, Admiral Television Corporation sponsored a booth at the Los Angeles County Fair in Pomona. Other television-manufacturing firms present were General Electric, RCA, Philco, Motorola and Zenith. I was assigned to make sure our display television sets were working at full capacity and answer the barrage of questions from fascinated visitors. I remember the many antennae and bits of coaxial cable scattered throughout the work areas. We were continually fiddling with the sets to present the very best pictures.

I also remember the first coast-to-coast black and white telecast in September 1951. President Harry Truman opened the Japanese Peace Treaty Conference in San Francisco. The conference concluded with a final agreement outlining the terms of peace for Japan. In 1952, another television hallmark took place with the first nationally televised Republican and Democratic National Conventions. And in 1954, the Pasadena Rose Bowl Parade was broadcast in color nationwide for the first time. Since then, television has become a powerful medium, affecting the way billions of people all over the world live their daily lives. I think I had a sense of television's potential early on, but it was still amazing to watch as it developed over the last 50 years.

In April of 1949, while driving between customers for

Admiral Television in the San Marino area of California, I clearly remember sirens blaring and watching as emergency vehicles passed me by. After a while, I continued on my way and soon discovered the focal point of the commotion. I parked my car a few blocks ahead of the crisis. Approaching by foot, I joined hundreds of curious onlookers. Emergency vehicles, heavy equipment and television crews were all gathered. Live television coverage of the tragedy was unfolding.

The breaking news story was the first of its kind on local television. A three-year-old girl by the name of Kathy Fiscus had fallen down an abandoned well while playing near her home. Her parents heard her crying and summoned rescue workers immediately. The rescue effort was first heard on the radio, followed later by the live local television coverage. The television broadcast continued for more than twenty-four hours. After more than two days of strenuous effort, rescuers finally reached Kathy by digging another well parallel to hers and digging through at the bottom. Sadly, she didn't survive. I remember wherever there was a television, people were gathered to monitor the crisis. We all hoped so much that she would make it. It was heart breaking for everyone when it was announced that little Kathy had not survived. I've noticed in our society that we will readily assemble great amounts of resources to rescue a little girl from an abandoned well, but we are often less willing to spend relatively few resources to prevent such a tragedy by filling the abandoned wells around us.

While still working for Admiral TV, I made a courtesy call to a new customer, Clyde Southwick in Alhambra, California. I showed Mr. Southwick how to make some minor adjustments for better definition on his brand new Admiral television set. We made some small talk and as I was getting into the car to leave, he asked me for my phone number. I didn't think much of it at the time. Sometime later, Mr. Southwick called to ask me about working for his firm, The Homelite

Corporation. I wasn't looking to change jobs. I liked working for Admiral Television.

Mr. Southwick was the Regional Manager for the Homelite Corporation of Port Chester, New York. Its products included two-cycle engine chainsaws, sump pumps, lightweight generators, floodlights and cement breakers. Its main customers were utility companies, municipalities, construction companies and trimming and tree removal businesses. Clyde Southwick was convinced I could successfully market Homelite products and offered me a sales position. After much discussion, Irene and I decided to give it a try. If it didn't work out, we concluded, I could always go back to electronics.

I went to work at Homelite's Regional Office in Los Angeles. My sales boundaries extended mostly through southern California and included all of Arizona. I vividly recall my first sale. It was a three-inch sump pump to the Bear Valley Water District. My responsibilities took me to the Imperial Valley and Arizona several times a year. Charlie Guernon was my Sales Manager. I soon became his assistant. I was doing fairly well and on occasion I took trips to the home office in Port Chester, New York.

Discussions about establishing a sub-regional office in Arizona began to surface. I was asked if I would be interested in transferring to Arizona to run the new office. Since Arizona was part of my sales district, I was familiar with the area. Business out of Arizona was light, but with a full time presence the potential for new sales was great. It was a challenge I felt ready for. I talked to Irene about the opportunity. For days we considered the pros and the cons. Finally, we concluded that it was worth a try. Once again, we concluded, I could always go back to the electronics field.

The next morning, I left for the office with the full intent of informing Mr. Southwick that I would accept the transfer. However, while driving to work, the idea of leaving

California weighed more heavily upon me. By the time I arrived, my mind was made up. If I was going to make it, I was going to make it in California. It was California or bust. I called Irene and gave her the news. She was delighted. Then I told Mr. Southwick. Irene had already called her folks about our decision to transfer to Arizona. Grandma and Grandpa Morales were disappointed and were already missing their grandchildren. They were greatly relieved when Irene called back and told them we were staying.

Like many of our other forks in the road, I believe the Ayalas took the right turn. Not long afterwards, Mr. Southwick announced his retirement. His replacement was an ambitious bright young man from the San Francisco Homelite Office. Changes were made with office personnel and things were never quite the same.

One hot summer evening, Irene and I went shopping in Pomona. While I was waiting for Irene outside a store, I felt a tap on my shoulder. A gentleman asked, "Are you Ruben Ayala?" He introduced himself as Bob Ritter. He told me he had been a sports reporter for the Pomona Progress Bulletin Newspaper when my brother Maury and I played ball for Chino High. He asked what we were doing. I told him about Maury and gave him a quick selling job on Homelite products.

Ritter explained he was with Farmers Insurance and Farmers had just come out with an excellent career program. He said that while new agents were in training they could draw $275 a month, plus 100% of the commissions they earned over draw. He said with my selling experience, I would be a natural.

I was at first intrigued and then convinced. A month later, I became a Farmers Insurance agent. I was assigned to Ontario, just a few miles away. About the same time, Bob Ellingwood, a World War II and Korean War veteran also joined Farmers. Bob later became the Mayor of Ontario. Working under a "Certificate of Convenience," Bob and I studied for our insurance agent's license under Stan Rowdon, the District Manager. We passed the license examination on the same day.

Farmers had an incentive program called the Toppers Club. An annual sales quota was announced for all agents, regardless of their areas of operation. Quotas were set for all lines from automobile coverage to life insurance. During the program year, if an agent was on schedule, on a quarterly basis, he was given incentive gifts. At the end of the year, agents meeting or exceeding the set quota became Toppers Club members. They and their spouses received all-expense paid vacations to places such as Mexico City, Las Vegas, Palm Springs and Hawaii. An agent from Oceanside and I were the only two Career Program agents who made the Toppers Club the first year. We were honored at a lunch with the Chairman of the Board of Farmers Insurance in his private dining room on Wilshire Boulevard. Over time, Irene and I enjoyed vacations to Mexico City, Palm Springs and Las Vegas, compliments of Farmers Insurance.

In 1954, I established the first Farmers Insurance Office in Chino and continued to be a member of the Toppers Club until I was elected to the San Bernardino County Board of Supervisors in 1966. A year later, I sold my Chino franchise to my friend, Bob Gray, former Chino Councilman. Bob Ellingwood, by this time, had left the insurance business and had successfully developed his talents in real estate.

Each job in my career has been an opportunity, preparing me for other opportunities. Some may call it luck. However, it's been my experience that luck is usually what happens when preparation meets opportunity and opportunity is met with hard work. Either way, I'm grateful.

CHAPTER FIVE

FROM PTA TO THE MAYOR'S OFFICE

When our sons Bud and Eddie were enrolled at Richard Gird Elementary School, Irene and I became involved in the PTA. We were elected to co-chair the Ways and Means Committee. In that capacity, I had some lively discussions with the school's Principal from time to time. She was noted for being rigid and unyielding and apparently she wasn't accustomed to parents challenging her views. However, I had no problem doing just that, albeit respectfully. At the time, I wasn't aware that other parents appreciated my standing up to her.

Early in 1955, I was mowing our front lawn when Garland Mendenhall, Vice Principal at Gird, came to visit. "Mendy" was a student at La Verne College when I was at Chino High. He had kept up with Maury and me through the local newspapers' sport pages. After some small talk, he told me he came by for a reason. Two members of the Chino School Board who were up for re-election had decided not to run again. Folks had approached Mendy to ask me if I might be interested in running.

My first reaction was, "You must be kidding." I had no idea what the responsibilities of the Board of Education were. Besides, I was too busy rearing our young family and working out of Los Angeles. I was spending most of my free time with our sons and their Little League Baseball team, which I enjoyed very much. Glen Monger and I managed and coached the 20-30 Team of the National League. Glen's son, John, who became a successful head football coach at Chino High, was our star pitcher. We won a number of championships.

I thanked Mendy for thinking about me, but, "No thanks!" was my reply. A week or so later, Mendenhall was back again. This time, he was armed with a petition signed by quite a few citizens, including many of my fellow PTA members. After talking it over with Irene, I decided to break new ground, and breaking new ground it was. I agreed to run for a position on the Board of Education for the Chino Unified School District.

I didn't know too much about the duites of the School Board. I knew even less about campaigning. There were seven candidates for just two openings. We had a fundraising dinner at the Chino Community Building, an all you can eat spaghetti blast ($1.00 for adults and $.75 for children). We had so much spaghetti left over that we spent the next morning giving it away to families in need. We had one candidates' debate, held at Newman Elementary School Auditorium. I can still remember most of my first political speech. Some members of the local Farm Bureau Chapter organized a strong campaign against the school board's building policy. I openly rejected their rationale and made one strong promise to voters, "To work to provide the best quality education for our students."

Ignacio Lopez, owner and publisher of El Espectador, a small bilingual newspaper in Pomona, became interested in my School Board race. He gave me the idea of naming block captains and giving them the responsibility for making sure all registered voters living in their neighborhood went to the polls. There were no controversial issues, except that the local chapter of the farm bureau opposed just about everything the school board did. Elsa Ross, who had been involved with the Newman School PTA, and I were elected. We were sworn in on July 1, 1955 and we were both re-elected without opposition four years later.

During my first term on the School Board, a group of Chino citizens, including two former School Board members, appeared before us at one of the School Board meetings. They presented a survey indicating that the illegal drug related problems in Chino, mostly associated with marijuana, were originating from the homes located south of Riverside Drive in an area often referred to as the Chino Barrio. They wanted the Board to disallow students who lived in those neighborhoods from attending Chino schools with the other students.

When they completed their presentation, Board President Reiley asked if any of the Board members had any questions or wished to respond. I indicated I did.

I responded that their concerns may be well founded, but since I wasn't yet privy to the details of their study used to support their allegations, I wouldn't be able to make a decision that night. Then I asked rhetorically, "Who are these people living in the Chino Barrio?" Answering my own question, I continued, "I will tell you who they are. They are the products of generations of ethnic isolation who have been compelled to live in a segregated environment, which over time, has had the effect of lowering their expectations. If you treat people like second-class citizens for decades, the odds are that at least some of them will live up to that expectattion. Some of you here tonight helped contribute to this problem and perhaps the chickens have come home to roost."

One of the former School Board members jumped to his feet, taking strong issue with my characterization of the situation. He said that it was nonsense that Chino schools had ever been segregated. He told the Board that separate schools for Mexican-Americans had been established for the convenience of the families living in the Chino Barrio. When he was finished, I defined segregation for him and told him how degrading and harmful it was. As a Board, we didn't take any action that night and the issue was never brought up again.

One paramount responsibility the School Board faces is selecting the most qualified superintendent available when a vacancy occurs. Two years into my term, we had to confront that task when Mr. Levi Dickey announced his intentions to retire. Some board members felt it would be wise to recruit on a nationwide basis. I was one of those who thought that it would be good for the morale of the district employees if we could find someone qualified from within the ranks. In the military service, poor morale was often the consequence when replacement personnel were brought in from outside our battalion.

The name of Gerald Litel, Principal of Chino High, surfaced. Board President Melvin "Mel" K. Reiley appointed me to meet with Mr. Litel and find out if he would be interested. His response was positive and the Board unanimously approved his selection.

Incidentally, Mr. Dickey and Mr. Litel both have schools named after them in the Chino Valley Unified School District. Levi Dickey Elementary School opened in 1981 and Gerald Litel Elementary School opened in 1987. During my term on the School Board, the new Chino High School Campus on Park Place was finally completed, with the addition of some new classrooms, a new library and a large swimming pool. Chino High School Memorial Field and Stadium was dedicated previously on October 20, 1950, four and half years before my election to the School Board. I clearly remember the first graduation ceremonies held at the stadium for the Class of 1951. For my high school classmates and me, it marked the ten-year anniversary of our graduation in 1941.

Anticipating growth in the Chino area, we acquired property for Glenmead Elementary (est. 1969), Walnut Avenue Elementary (est. 1969), Los Serranos Elementary (est. 1963), E.J. Marshall Elementary (est. 1964) and Ramona Jr. High (est. 1965). Although the schools weren't built until after my tenure on the School Board, we felt it was necessary to prepare the way. We also authorized the demolition of the original Gird

Elementary School, which had been designated unsafe due to seismic problems. Because of traffic problems caused by high school students during lunch break, we closed the campus during school hours to all students except seniors. Many high school students and parents were upset with the decision, but I believe safety concerns warranted it.

When it came to hiring faculty members, Superintendent Dickey strongly recommended we open the hiring to the best-qualified credentialed applicants. On his good advice, we hired Mr. Reuben Sam Burton, the first African American teacher in the Chino Unified School District. He went on to become an outstanding administrator. Mr. Reiley, a Chino High School graduate, was our Board President and was succeeded by William Ingram, a poultry rancher.

In early 1962, my friend John Ingrao, Sr. came into my insurance office. John was a Captain with the Chino Police Reserves. I thought he had just come by for a visit, but it turned out to be more than just a chat. He presented me with a petition signed by Chino citizens, soliciting me to enter the Chino City Council race. Councilman Robert Gray had announced that he would not seek re-election.

I was enjoying my second term on the Chino School Board. I was by then quite familiar and comfortable with school district issues. While I was aware of some city issues, I would have to do some homework to be fully prepared. I was faced with a dilemma. This time, Irene left the decision entirely up to me. After careful consideration, I decided to make a run for one of the open seats on the Chino City Council.

I submitted my candidate's paperwork to City Clerk Ernie Wangler, just a few minutes before closing time on the day it was due. Although the City Council race involved less registered voters than the School Board election, it carried more public interest and intensity. I was soon made aware of some backroom meetings and maneuvers taking place.

Retiring Councilman Bob Gray endorsed me, which helped my campaign immensely. There were nine candidates running for the three Council seats, which included incumbents Carl Schuler and Zeke Cortez. With some experience in campaigning under my belt, we organized the Ayala for City Council Campaign Committee. There were several debates sponsored by the local Chamber of Commerce. I don't recall any grand statements being made by any of the candidates. Not one candidate spoke about the proposed construction of a freeway through Chino, which would later hugely impact the growth of the Chino Valley.

It was a typical city election. On the phones, candidates and their supporters reminded as many as possible to get out and vote. Transportation was provided to those requesting it. Once Election Day was officially over, the counting of the votes was under way. Our camp enjoyed the entire evening. Right from the start, I was in the lead and never lost it. Finally, with all precincts reporting, I received more votes than any other candidate, including the two incumbents, who were both re-elected. They were pleased to get re-elected, but disappointed in my higher vote count. One incumbent told a reporter that I was the top vote getter because teachers in the School District were so disenchanted with me as a School Board member that they all decided to vote for me for City Councilman, so that they could get rid of me. The truth is, many teachers expressed their disappointment in my departure from the School Board. Ever so often, I wear the Bulova watch presented to me at my last School Board Meeting. The back is engraved, "Ruben S. Ayala, in appreciation from CTA 1962." It still keeps me on time.

Irene's uncle, Andrew Morales, preceded me as a Chino City Councilman. In fact, he was the first Chino citizen of Mexican heritage to be elected to the Chino City Council. He served two full terms from 1946 to 1954. During that time he worked at Morales Market, owned by Irene's parents.

Andrew "Andy" Morales was an honest and decent city official who served with dignity at a time when minority elected officials throughout the State of California were almost non-existent. It can be said, without fear of contradiction, that Andy opened the door for other Chino Latino leaders who followed such as Zeke Cortez, Ralph Preciado, Pete Garcia, Angel Martinez, Martin Salgado, Leo Leon, Agustine Tapia, Louie Moreno and yes, Ruben Ayala. I remember one afternoon at a family gathering shortly after I returned home from military service when Andy approached me and after some casual conversation suggested that I seriously consider getting involved in city politics. I was still in school and my aspirations were far removed from city politics. I thanked him for the consideration, but told him I didn't have any interest and probably wouldn't have any interest in the future. Little did I suspect how time and circumstances would prove me so wrong.

What happened in the days following the City Council election is the reason it is essential that the Brown Act, requiring open meetings, be fully enforced. In 1962, the Chino City Council members selected the City Mayor, supposedly on a rotation basis. However, the Mayor was chosen and remained only at the whim of his or her colleagues. The Mayor could be removed from this honor at any time. All four of the other councilmen wanted to be the Mayor. They were divided into two camps. Councilmen Carl Anderson and Zeke Cortez were in one camp and Councilmen Carl Schuler and F. W. Rhodehouse were in the other. It became obvious that I would be the swing vote. The first to call me to set up a meeting was the Anderson-Cortez team. They checked with City Attorney Charlie Warner, who counseled them that since I had not yet been sworn in, the three of us could meet without violating the Brown Act. This is no longer the case.

We took a drive into the countryside. When I wouldn't commit myself to a choice for Mayor, Anderson said that he would yield to Cortez on the strength that Zeke was a native son of Chino, just like himself. Zeke was also the second in seniority on the Council. Anderson was the senior member and as such felt that I should support Zeke. They thought my support for Zeke was needed. They dropped me off at my insurance office with the expectation that I would seriously consider Zeke Cortez as Mayor.

A day or so after my ride with Anderson and Cortez, Carl Schuler phoned, wanting to meet with me. He and Councilman F. W. Rhodehouse wanted to discuss an important issue. We met at Schuler's home on Monte Vista Avenue. Schuler had decided to support Rhodehouse for Mayor and wanted to know if they could count on my support. As the meeting concluded, I told them that I hadn't made up my mind.

It was a crowded City Council Chamber the night of my first City Council Meeting. The City Clerk conducted the meeting until the Mayor was selected. Right after we were sworn in, Tony Peich and Bob Gray presented Mr. Wangler with a petition. Unbeknownst to me, they had been out circulating the petition, asking the City Council to name me as Mayor since I had received more votes than the others. Mr. Wangler thanked both Tony and Bob, set the petition aside and it was never addressed again. Councilman Anderson immediately nominated Zeke Cortez and moved that nominations be closed. The motion failed. Schuler then nominated Councilman Rhodehouse for Mayor and also moved that nominations be closed. The motion carried and a vote was taken for Mayor. The winning vote was 3-2 in favor of Zeke Cortez. I cast the deciding vote.

I had known Zeke since I was a youngster. As a matter of fact, he was born just three houses north of where I was born. He was a Chino High graduate, Class of 1931, and a long-time businessman. I knew Zeke was honest. I met Rhodehouse for the first time at our meeting at Schuler's home. I voted for Cortez, but often wondered what kind of a stalemate I would have caused, if I had abstained. How would the City Council have proceeded with a 2-2 vote?

During the same meeting, Lloyd Allen, one of the previous nine candidates for City Council, asked the City Attorney how one could go about having the voters elect the Mayor directly instead of having the City Council do it. The City Attorney explained the process to make the change. I supported the concept, but my colleagues, by their silence, indicated they didn't care for the idea.

In another City Council meeting, supporters of mine appeared before the Council to voice their displeasure with what they considered a fast shuffle and total disregard of their petition to name me as Mayor. They respectfully urged the City Council to place a measure on the next election ballot, whereby the voters would be granted the right to directly elect their Mayor. A long and sometimes heated discussion ensued. Most City Council members didn't want to give up their opportunity to become an appointed Mayor or the power to elect the Mayor themselves. At the end, the City Council grudgingly agreed. The City Attorney was instructed to draw up the language and the ballot measure was scheduled for the next election, two years later.

Some days later, Mayor Cortez called me to tell me he was in the process of appointing Chair positions to City Committees. He wanted me to come over to his home and discuss the appointments. When I arrived, he readily advised me that the most important committees would be assigned according to seniority. There was no discussion. He told me I would be appointed as Chairman of the Recreation and Education Committee. Since the City of Chino had no parks, he said, "You aren't going to be very busy. You are Chairman of a nothing committee."

I went home and shared the conversation with Irene. I remember telling her that the Mayor had given me a bunch of lemons and I was going to make the best lemonade in town. The Mayor was right about one thing; we had no parks in Chino. I set out to organize a Citizens' Committee of Chino residents interested in promoting parks. Gretchen McCombs was the leader of the group. We discussed various approaches to developing parks throughout Chino. We developed detailed plans of different park configurations and locations. Within six months, we were ready to present our plans to the City Council. We would divide the City area into quarters. Riverside Drive and Central Avenue were the dividing boundaries. Each quarter section would have a three-acre neighborhood park, with a Little League field. Then we would ask the California Department of Corrections to lease to the city a 60-acre parcel of unused California Institution for Men (CIM) property located at the southeast corner of Edison and Central. We would float a $130,000 park bond issue to cover the initial construction. The City Council approved our plan.

I went to Sacramento and met with my friend, Assemblyman John Quimby, who, without hesitation, agreed to carry the resolution regarding the lease of CIM's surplus property to our city for a park. The resolution passed, indicating the lease would be approved only if the people of Chino approved the bond issue. The bond measure received support from the majority of voters, but failed to meet the minimum two-thirds requirement. After the election, the debate continued. Most people recognized the need for neighborhood parks, but had reservations about a park so close to the prison.

After more meetings with the Citizens Park Committee, we decided to try another ballot measure. This time, we gave the voters the option of voting for the four neighborhood parks or the 60-acre park on the Institution grounds. We thought it was an effective compromise. Unfortunately, the second ballot measure also failed to meet the minimum two-thirds requirement. It wasn't until I was a State Senator that we were able to get the State to lease the 60-acre parcel without any conditions attached. While I may have started out as the "Chairman of a nothing committee," we began what became an assertive and productive parks program in the City of Chino that continues to this day.

Two years after supporters had worked so hard to have the City Council name me Mayor, I felt obligated to enter the first Mayor's race. The ballot measure had passed and the voters of Chino were given the power to elect their own Mayor. There were three candidates: Incumbent Mayor Zeke Cortez, a local nursery owner named James Bruno and me, "the Chairman of a nothing committee." Mr. Bruno had the support of the Rotary Club, which included most of the prominent local businessmen. Predictions were that Zeke and I would split the Mexican-American vote and Mr. Bruno would gather most of the remaining 75% of the electorate. We had one debate in which Mr. Bruno and his supporters exuded much confidence. Someone from the audience even referred to Mr. Bruno as Mr. Mayor.

Mayor Cortez didn't run an aggressive campaign. Mr. Bruno criticized the leadership of the City and asked why the City officials hadn't done something about the deterioration of the town. I responded to Mr. Bruno that I certainly concurred with his observation and that we should start with his nursery on the southeast corner of Central and Walnut. It really was a shabby looking operation.

Mr. Bruno had also started his presentation by asking us to bow our heads while he led us in prayer. Since he wasn't noted for being a religious person, some doubted his sincerity. Our camp was grateful and encouraged by the endorsement of the local newspaper, the Chino Champion. Al McCombs, its publisher, was a member of the Chino Rotary Club, as were Mayor Cortez and Jim Bruno. We were delighted and heartily welcomed Mr. McCombs' endorsement, despite the disapproval of some of his fellow Rotarians.

With each election, we gained more experience. For this election, not only did we have a campaign committee, but we also organized an "Ayala for Mayor" Headquarters. We had lawn signs. Mailers went out to every voter. My supporters called registered voters every day in an attempt to get them to vote and suppoprt our campaign. After each name on the call list, volunteers noted: A for Ayala, B for Bruno, C for Cortez, or U for undecided. On Election Day, we made certain that everyone with an A next to their name made it to the polls. Then we concentrated on voters with a U after their names.

On April 21, 1964, I became the first Mayor in the history of Chino directly elected by the voters. After I was sworn in, we named Joe Ames, a successful Chino businessman, to fill my Council seat. Ames, in my opinion, was one of the most astute individuals to ever serve on the Chino City Council.

As Mayor, I felt the open area south of Schaefer and west of Central Avenue would be best developed as an industrial park. After building a consensus, we installed a large size pipeline along the south side of Schaefer, running west of Central Avenue, to handle larger amounts of industrial waste. Warehousing was later built in the area and our investment paid off.

It wasn't too long into my tenure when I became painfully aware that the west end of San Bernardino County was badly lacking acute and emergency medical services. Two youngsters, one accidentally shot by a younger brother and a little girl hit by a car on Third and D streets, died without any local emergency medical services. I made it a priority to remedy the tragedy. I lobbied hard for the County to provide a satellite County emergency hospital to the Chino area.

At a joint City and County Meeting, I debated with Supervisor Chairman Ross Dana, Sr. about the need for local emergency medical services in Chino. He contended that the west end of the County already had County services at the intersection of the I-10 Freeway and Mountain Avenue in Ontario. I agreed that we could obtain building permits and the like at that location as well as go to trial there, but that we didn't have access to emergency medical services at that location. I stated that I believed the County had its priorities confused. For the protection of life and limb, we had to travel 30 miles from our city. I also wrote to every county in the State requesting information on how they handled their emergency cases in outlying areas. Many counties responded and a lot of regional interest was generated.

In the midst of the publicity, John Setlich, a local land developer, approached me with a plan to build a hospital in Chino. John and his family were good friends of my family. John wanted to build the hospital according to State specifications in order to qualify for State maintained indigent patients. It would be his first hospital construction project. John and I met a number of times with financial consultants. The parcel of land he was looking at was north of Philadelphia on the west side of Central Avenue, generally where Pep Boys is located today. Then, unexpectedly, I received a call from the CEO of a company with offices in the southern part of the United States. He told me his company had "wheel-barrels full of money" and that they wanted to build the hospital. They had experience building several hospitals in California and were familiar with the State's strict requirements. They knew how to maneuver through the bureaucracy. Meanwhile, John Setlich was delayed by red tape and was unable to get the project off the ground.

Ultimately, we decided to move forward with the other company's proposal and began the approval process for con-

struction. The hospital, known today as the Chino Valley
Medical Center, on Walnut east of Central Avenue, was officially opened in October of 1972. Not only did the Chino Valley
end up with emergency medical services, but acute health services, as well. The facility has been expanded over the years to
meet increasing demand.

Automobile curb parking along Riverside Drive became
a serious safety problem during my time as Mayor. After meetings with Police Chief David Pruitt and City Engineer Ed
Lynch, we decided that since the City didn't have the financial
capability to purchase the right-of-way to widen the street, we
would propose to the City Council that all curb parking along
Riverside Drive be prohibited. Merchants with businesses and
residents living along Riverside Drive protested vigorously. On
a split vote, the motion to prohibit parking on Riverside Drive
passed.

As Mayor, I was a member of the Pomona Freeway
Association. Established in October of 1961, its members
included representatives from the cities directly affected by the
proposed construction of the Pomona Freeway from Monterey
Park to Riverside. Its purpose was to work with the California
Department of Highways in the careful planning and construction of the Pomona Freeway.

In the late 1950's, the City of Chino established a
Citizens' Committee on Freeway Routing. Al McCombs, the
publisher of the Chino Champion newspaper, was its
Chairman. Working closely with then City Administrator Dick
Wright, the Committee proposed to the Chino City Council
several alternative routes for the Pomona Freeway through
Chino. The City Council then forwarded its preferred proposal
to the California Department of Highways through the
Pomona Freeway Association. It proposed that as the eastbound freeway route reached Reservoir Avenue that it swerve
southward until it paralleled Schaefer Avenue. It would then

continue along Schaefer Avenue until swooping northward at
Euclid to resume its current eastbound course. The rationale
was that the area along Schaefer Avenue was much less populated, with fewer people and structures to relocate.

The California Department of Highways rejected the
Chino City Council's proposal, choosing instead the more direct
existing route, which parallels Philadelphia Avenue. As a con-
cession, Chino was granted its further request to have the
Pomona Freeway submerged rather than elevated. I strongly
supported the idea of submerging the Pomona Freeway to protect the property values along the freeway and enhance the freeway driving experience through Chino. The City Council was
also concerned that a level or elevated freeway would create a
"Chinese Wall" and divide the city as it grew to the north, creating a North Chino and a South Chino. In January of 1971,
the portion of the Pomona Freeway through Chino to Euclid
Avenue was completed, initiating a continual wave of growth in
the Chino Valley.

Due to the tremendous growth in the Inland Empire
brought about in part by the extended completion of the
Pomona Freeway on to Riverside and beyond, remedies are
being sought to ameliorate the more frequent heavy traffic on
the freeway. Most recently, discussions have focused on constructing a raised second level for truck use only. Commercial
trucking has grown tremendously over the last decade, as the
Pomona Freeway has become the preferred thoroughfare for
truckers between L.A. and Orange Counties and Riverside and
San Bernardino Counties.

CHAPTER SIX

ON TO COUNTY SUPERVISOR

After years at Chino City Hall, I had yet to meet our
San Bernardino County Supervisor, Paul Young. I met with his
field representative a number of times, but Supervisor Young
didn't spend much time in our end of the district. I think he
spent most of his time in the Colton area where his home was
and where he had previously served as Mayor.

One morning, we were both attending a groundbreaking ceremony for the Central Avenue overpass over the
Southern Pacific Railroad tracks between Holt and Mission in
the City of Montclair. Supervisor Young repeatedly mentioned
how pleased he was to finally get the Mountain Avenue overpass started. His field representative kept trying to get his
attention to tell him that we were on Central Avenue, not on
Mountain Avenue. He finally realigned his bearings.

Sometime later I was visiting with Montclair Mayor
Harold Hayes. We were disappointed that Supervisor Young
seldom made an appearance in the west end of the county and
when he did he was not familiar with the area. I suggested to
Mayor Hayes that he consider running for Supervisor from our
district. He said he would take my suggestion under advise-
ment, but he would run only if Supervisor Young didn't seek
re-election. Young decided to run.

This time, there were no petitions urging me to enter

the race. On my own, I decided the west end of San Bernardino County was seriously lacking representation at the County Seat. Since Mayor Hayes indicated he would not oppose Supervisor Young, I decided to take the giant step. Earnie Smith, who with his brother Chuck operated the Chevron Station at the corner of Central and Riverside in Chino, took a leave of absence to help run my campaign. Earnie became second in command to Jay Rodriguez, my campaign manager. They had their work cut out for them as my name recognition beyond Chino was practically non-existent.

There were five candidates for the County Supervisor seat: Young, the incumbent; Mel Fuchs, a realtor and former Colton Mayor; Robert Sherer, a Deputy Sheriff and strawberry farmer; Gordon (Gordy) Young, a former Fontana School Board member; and Ruben S. Ayala, the mayor of Chino. The one advantage I had was that I was the only one running from the West End. My highest priority was to meet as many new people as possible on a daily basis. I held a press conference in Fontana, but it didn't go as smoothly as I hoped.

At my first campaign meeting in Colton, I made a new friend, Pasqual Oliva, the Mayor of Colton. I had played baseball and basketball for Chino High against Pasqual when he attended Colton High. We didn't really know each other then, but I remembered that in baseball he was a tough pitcher. This time, we hit it off. Mayor Oliva had already committed to endorsing Mel Fuchs, but he graciously introduced me to some of his friends, who, in turn, introduced me to their friends throughout the District. I received substantial support and encouragement from a newfound constituency. Earnie Smith and I traversed the Fourth Supervisorial District time and time again, meeting and speaking to hundreds of residents. Within two months, my name recognition had increased dramatically.

Two public debates were held. Supervisor Young often appeared bewildered by so much opposition to his re-election;

however, to his credit, the Supervisor always maintained a dig-
nified and respectful demeanor. Supervisor Young and Gordy
Young leased billboard space throughout the Fourth District,
promoting their separate candidacies. Initially, our camp just
didn't have the finances and when we finally did the billboard
people told us we were too late. All the locations in the district
had been leased out. Instead, we produced a number of attrac-
tive mailers, designed by Jay Rodriguez, our campaign manager.

After months of campaigning, the primary election was
held on June 7, 1966. With all precincts reporting, I received
7,689 votes and incumbent Supervisor Young received 6,285
votes. The rest of the votes were distributed among the other
three candidates. Lacking over 50% of the total votes cast, I
would have to face Supervisor Young in the General Election
on November 8, 1966.

I immediately contacted the three unsuccessful candidates for their endorsements. Mel Fuchs and Gordy Young,
without hesitation, agreed to endorse me. Robert Sherer played
hard-to-get and eventually came out in support of Supervisor
Young. Gordy and Mel not only endorsed my candidacy in the
General Election, but actively promoted me along with many of
their constituents.

As the General Election drew closer, the San
Bernardino County Grand Jury issued a scathing report. The
report accused the Board of Supervisors of squandering public
funds at Park Moabi, a County Regional Park, located in
Needles. Earnie Smith and I drove to Needles and spent days
making inquiries regarding the Grand Jury accusations. We
returned home with enough evidence to convince us that the
Board of Supervisors had, indeed, blown a well-intended project. We mentioned the County's lack of interest in providing
emergency services to outlying areas and the Park Moabi fiasco
every time we had the opportunity.

During the period between the Primary and the General

Election, Supervisor Young lost his son. Out of respect for
him and his family, I called for a ten-day moratorium on any
campaigning by our camp.

November 8, 1966 was a typical election day with all of
the get-out-the-vote activity and usual excitement connected
with an election. After the polls were closed, the ballots started
to trickle in. I trailed at first, but not by much. Mel Fuchs,
who had joined us to follow the returns, shook my hand and
congratulated me on my victory. I asked Mel, "How can you
congratulate me when I'm behind in the vote count?" He
answered, "Well, I checked with the Registrar of Voters Office
and all the votes counted so far are from Supervisor Young's
home area. Wait till they start counting the West End ballots.
Congratulations, Supervisor Ayala!"

Mel's observation was right on target. When the final
count was over, I had received 17,923 votes against Supervisor
Young's 13,803 votes. I was sworn in as the Fourth District
Supervisor of the San Bernardino County Board of
Supervisors on December 6, 1966. Four years later, I was re-
elected without opposition.

As a County Supervisor, it didn't take me long to notice
that the inclination and attitude of some of the Board members was clearly in favor of downtown San Bernardino. The
decision making barometer seemed to be that if a County decision was good for downtown San Bernardino then it was good
for the entire County. San Bernardino County was and is today
the largest county in the United States with significant needs
throughout the entire county and not just in downtown San
Bernardino.

I based my observation on the disproportional amount
of phone calls and visits I received from County-elected officials and business people from the city of San Bernardino. The
judges, Sheriff, District Attorney and various influential business people had much too much to say about how the rest of

13157 2nd St. Chino, CA – Ruben's birthplace, where it all began, March 6, 1922. The house still stands.

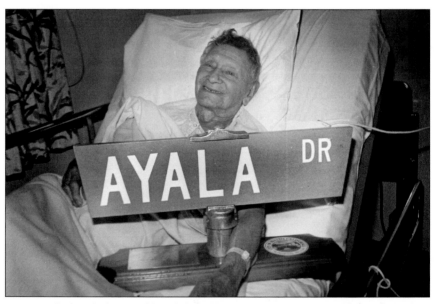

1981 – Ruben's father, Mauricio, with a street sign presented to Senator Ayala by the City of Rialto. He passed away shortly thereafter. This was his last picture – taken at The Chino Valley Medical Center.

Ruben's beloved Aunt Esther passed away at age 100 in 2000.

Top row from left to right: Ruben, Ruben's father Mauricio and brother Maury. Bottom row from left to right: sisters Rosina, Susie and Estella.

1939 – Chino High School varsity basketball team. From left to right: Karl Johnson, Ruben Ayala, Ralph Garcia & Paul Abbot.

December 1940 – from left to right: Cheerleader Barbara Meairs, Captain Ruben Ayala, Cheerleader Marcia McConnell, Paul Bernard and Coach Levi Dickey.

Circa 1941 – Ruben Ayala of Pomona Junior College shoots and scores against Chaffey Junior College as his teamates, Louie Robinson (13) and Forrest Black (17), watch.

1942 – Marcie Morales - third from left, bottom row. Ruben S. Ayala - second from left, second row from top.

In 1942 Ruben enlisted in the United States Marine Corps. He saw action in the South Pacific while serving with the First Marine Division. He was honorably discharged in 1946.

1945 – From Left to Right: Ruben S. Ayala, C.M. Ayala and "The Chick" Williamson at Klamath Falls, Oregon.

Circa 1944 – Ruben and Irene's first date at Hollywood's famous Earl Carroll's restaurant shortly after Ruben's return from the South Pacific. Earl Carroll's was one of the places to go in those days. It is no longer in existence.

Irene's senior photo. Chino High School class of 1942, where she excelled scholastically and athletically.

July 1947 – Irene graduated from the California Hospital School of Nursing in Los Angeles, Ca.

1947 – Ruben and Irene standing in front of Moore Hall, nurses' residence, on Irene's graduation day from The California Hospital School of Nursing and the University of Southern California.

July 1945 – Ruben and Irene's wedding day. From left to right: Ring Bearer Roman Vasquez (front), Maid of Honor Mary L. Morales, Bride Irene M. Ayala, Groom Ruben S. Ayala and Best Man Marcie Morales.

1950 – Christmas in Chino with Grandpa Morales and family pets.

Irene and Ruben with two of their sons, Maurice (left) and Bud (right). Gary was born in 1952.

May 1955 – From left to right: Gary, Ruben, Bud, Irene & Maurice.

Bud, Maurice & Gary Ayala

Circa 1955 – Newspaper ad for school board campaign. First ever political newspaper advertisement.

1960 – Chino School Board. From left to right: William Ingram, Ruben S. Ayala, President Elsa Ross, Henrie John & Bob McLeod, who succeeded Ruben as Mayor of Chino in 1965.

Circa 1963 – Ruben S. Ayala, Chino's first elected Mayor.

1966 – Supervisor Ayala in front of the S.B. County Courthouse
(photo by Jay Rodriguez)

December 2, 1968 – Supervisor Dan Mikesell, as outgoing Chairman of the Board, presenting Ruben S. Ayala the gavel as the new Chairman of the Board. From left to right: Supervisors Donald Beckord, Daniel Mikesell, Chairman Ruben S. Ayala, Nancy Smith and William Betterley.

1968 – San Bernardino County Board of Supervisors. From left to right: Donald Beckord (3rd District), Daniel D. Mikesell (2nd Distrct), Ruben S. Ayala, Chairman (4th District), Nancy E. Smith (5th District), and William Betterley (1st district).

Visiting Bud during Basic Training at Fort Ord, Ca. From left to right:
Gary, Ruben, Irene, Bud & Maurice

Irene, at Fort Ord, wearing son Bud's Army jacket.

April 18, 1973 – Demolition of the old Chino City Hall to make room for the present library and a city/county complex with funds provided by the Joint Powers Authority, which Ruben initiated as County Supervisor.

1982 – Ruben and Irene at the dedication of the City of Chino's Ruben S. Ayala Community Park; with Mayor Larry Walker assisting.

1985 – Ruben and Irene celebrating 40 years of marriage.

Daughters of Gary Ayala, Sarah Rose Ayala (left) and Amy Elizabeth Ayala (right), ages 16 and 13, respectively, of Rancho Santa Margarita, Ca.

Ruben and Irene at the dedication of Ruben S. Ayala Community Park. In the background is his father's 1954 Chevy, which is still in the family.

1988 – Ayala High School groundbreaking ceremony. Chino Unified School District board members from left to right: Gary Borcharding, Dena Beno, Ruben S. Ayala (Senator), Harold Nelms (President) and Donna Silva.

Ruben and his granddaughter, Danielle Ayala, prior to the construction of Ayala High School. Danielle is Maurice's daughter.

Ruben and Irene with the school plaque at the dedication of Ayala High School.

State Sen. Ruben Ayala, D-34th District, speaks at assembly during first day of classes Tuesday at Chino Hills high school that bears his name.

Ayala High students 'on the ground floor'

By Paul Hughes
Bulletin Staff Writer

State Sen. Ruben Ayala on Tuesday urged 1,000 students at a new school bearing his name to take education seriously and be proud that they are "in on the ground floor of tradition."

As several schools throughout the Inland Valley opened for the new year

name in print before, but to see it on a school . . . I think it will take six months to sink in.

In a 40-minute morning assembly, Ayala told students to be proud that they are beginning a new tradition, to take school seriously and to steer clear of drugs. A San Bernardino County Sheriff's Department helicopter hovered overhead bearing a banner that

Portion of a newspaper article about the first day of classes at AHS.

1993 – Ruben S. Ayala on the cover of Bulldog Life magazine with some of the first graduates of AHS.

1967 – From left to right: Supervisor Ruben S. Ayala, L.A. County Supervisor Pete Schabarum and the late Montclair Mayor Harold Hayes discuss Ruben's proposal for a San Bernardino to Los Angeles commuter train, currently known as the Metro-Link.

1976 – California Senator Ruben S. Ayala introducing a legislative measure on the Senate floor.

June 21, 1974 – A newspaper clipping showing Gov. Ronald Reagan signing a bill introduced by State Sen. Ruben S. Ayala.

Circa 1982 – Governor Jerry Brown and State Senator Ruben S. Ayala discussing the senator's proposal to construct the "Peripheral Canal", enabling the transfer of northern California water to southern California.

California Senator Ruben S. Ayala discussing the Peripheral Canal with Ron Robie, California Director of Water Resources. Note: Robie is now a Superior Court Judge in Sacramento.

Governor Jerry Brown signs Senator Ayala's Senate Bill 200 (Peripheral Canal Bill).

Ruben and Irene at the White House with President Gerald Ford and Jay Rodriguez (background).

Senator Ruben S. Ayala at the White House with President Jimmy Carter.

Senator Ruben S. Ayala with the late Congressman George Brown and President Bill Clinton.

Senator Ruben S. Ayala at the White House with House Speaker Tip O'Neil.

Assemblyman Fred Aguiar appears on Senator Ruben S. Ayala's cable television show, "Up Front with Senator Ayala".

Insurance Commissioner John Garamendi appears on Senator Ruben S. Ayala's cable television show, "Up Front with Senator Ayala".

the County was governed. To the distress of some officials, I became Chairman of the Board of Supervisors in 1968 and continued in that capacity until 1972.

As Board Chairman, I had some interesting interactions with many of the officials I mentioned. On one occasion, Sheriff Bland became so frustrated when I wouldn't support him on a fiscal matter that he put his nose up to mine. He bellowed, "I've heard about you! Your problem is that you're an ex-Marine with a Mexican temper." While he was still in my face, I answered just as loudly, "And you're an ex-Marine with an Irish temper, so what is your problem?" After a healthy exchange of mutual concerns, Sheriff Bland and I eventually became good friends.

As Supervisor, I vigorously supported flood control projects throughout San Bernardino County, including the controversial Mentone Dam proposal, which later became the Seven Oaks Dam Project near Mentone. Completed on November 15, 1999, the dam was built to protect downstream cities such as Redlands and Loma Linda, which in the past had suffered from severe flooding during heavy rains. Constructed by the U.S. Army Corps of Engineers, San Bernardino County was required to provide just 1% of the total $250 million price tag. Orange County paid 38%, Riverside County paid 2% and the U.S. Congress allocated the remaining 59%. For San Bernardino County, the Seven Oaks Dam Project turned out to be a great benefit at a relatively low cost. I believe it was well worth the effort.

Supervisor Dan Mikesell, as Chairman of the Board, initiated the creation of the Prado County Regional Park near Chino, located behind an earlier dam project completed in 1941, the Prado Dam. As Chairman, I advanced the Prado Regional Park project almost to completion. It covered over 2,000 acres. Supervisor Robert Townsend, appointed to replace me when I was elected to the State Senate, succeeded in putting the finishing touches on one of the finest parks in our region. In 2003, the area around and including Prado Regional Park officially became a part of the City of Chino. San Bernardino County continues to manage the Park, while the U.S. Army Corps of Engineers maintains ownership of the land.

As Chairman of the Board of Supervisors, I was successful in creating a Joint Powers Authority between San Bernardino County and the City of Chino, resulting in the construction of the current San Bernardino County Branch Library in Chino, the Chino City Hall, the Chino Police Station, and the San Bernardino County Courthouse in Chino. The buildings are all located together in a government center on the corner of Chino Avenue and Central Avenue. Under the Joint Powers Authority, the City of Chino was able to acquire the investment funds needed at favorable loan rates with the County Government guaranteeing the financing. I was delighted to recently be informed by members of the Joint Powers Authority Board, Chairman Dr. Bruce Lensch and Frances Rodelo, who I had originally appointed, that the last payment has been made. It appears that the Joint Powers Authority has successfully carried out its obligation to the great benefit of the City of Chino.

One of my earlier involvements as a new County Supervisor was to reinvigorate the long neglected Water Works #8 in the Chino Hills Sleepy Hollow area. The Water Works #8 was supposed to be a local advisory board established to provide valuable management expertise to the County concerning local water supply issues. The problem was we couldn't find any record of who my predecessor had appointed or whether or not the advisory board continued to function. In response, I asked the County Board of Supervisors to declare all existing appointments (if any) vacated and allow me to select a new set of appointees. They agreed. I immediately appointed Jim Neller as Chairman. Jim was an excellent organizer and

very savvy when it came to underground potable water supplies
and management. Under Jim's leadership, Water Works #8
became a well run advisory committee for the proper management of local water supplies.

Karen Bristow, a long time resident and activist in the
Chino Hills area, recently informed me that Water Works #8 is
now under the jurisdiction of the City of Chino Hills. It's
good to know that Water Works #8 laid the foundation for the
reliable quality water supply now enjoyed by the residents of
the City of Chino Hills.

In my commute to and from my office in San
Bernardino, I would see the Southern Pacific trains loaded with
ore from Eagle Mountain in Riverside County, traveling to the
former Kaiser Steel Mill in Fontana. The train cars would later
return empty to Eagle Mountain. I asked County staff to
research the feasibility of contracting with Southern Pacific to
load the returning empty train cars with household refuse and
deposit it in the three huge holes created by the ore mining at
Eagle Mountain. I thought that the three huge holes could take
care of the County's excess disposal filling needs for the next
hundred years. Unfortunately, the feasibility report indicated it
would be too expensive. Nevertheless, the amount of residential waste continues to grow, while the solutions are more and
more limited.

During my service as County Supervisor, there was a lot
of talk about constructing a high-speed passenger train system
from Ontario to Las Vegas, covering the distance in one hour.
I wasn't in favor of sending our residents and their money to
Las Vegas in just one hour and didn't support the idea. I was
never convinced that the Ontario-Las Vegas High Speed Train
would ever add any value to San Bernardino County or my
District.

I was much more concerned about the crowded traffic
conditions to and from people's work. In response, I advocated

for the construction of a commuter light rail system from San Bernardino to Los Angeles and back. I thought it would provide the best alternative to automobile travel for commuters and visitors.

As Board Chairman, I named a Commuter Train Committee to propose the best methods to develop the project. Committee Members were Montclair Mayor Harold Hayes; William Leonard, Sr., a train enthusiast from San Bernardino and a member of the California Transportation Commission; Eileen Carter, an outstanding Chino City Councilwoman; and a representative from Southern Pacific Railroad. I met with Los Angeles Mayor Tom Bradley and Los Angeles County Supervisor Pete Schabarum to discuss the venture. They were very much in favor. Our first challenge was to persuade one of the three railroad companies with a rail right-of-way from San Bernardino to Los Angeles to cooperate. After initial discussions with each of them, the Southern Pacific, Santa Fe and Union Pacific Railroad companies all showed interest. The Southern Pacific Railroad Company owned the most direct route, but had difficulty sandwiching passenger trains into its freight schedule. Then there was the problem of how to disperse arriving passengers at the Union Station in Los Angeles to their workplaces. The Committee dealt with many issues and continued through the lengthy process until the commuter rail system, the Metrolink, finally opened for passengers in October of 1992.

A comprehensive plan for the Metrolink project was just getting under way when I was elected to the State Senate. Still committed to the idea, I tried to meet with the Committee when I came home on weekends. The Committee felt the project was moving forward, but that it needed more attention than I could offer due to my other responsibilities with the Senate. In response, I contacted Supervisor Larry Walker, then President of the San Bernardino Associated Governments

(SANBAG) and suggested his organization take over the much-needed supervision, but only if they would give a high priority to work already completed by the Committee and continue the momentum the Committee had initiated. Supervisor Walker agreed and kept his word and due in large measure to his effective leadership, today, we have a superb commuter rail system. Running between the City of San Bernardino and Union Station in Los Angeles, the Metrolink boasts over 10,000 riders a day during the week with plans to expand further east to Redlands.

On January 11, 1972, the first civilian air-control tower at Chino County Airport was dedicated. Arvin O. Basnight, Western Regional Director for the Federal Aviation Administration, told those in attendance that Chino's 58-foot tower was the first of sixty-four towers to be constructed across the United States. Chino's tower was originally scheduled for completion in 1973. Thanks to my fellow Supervisors, who joined me in a well-targeted lobbying effort, the Chino air-control tower was given top priority and completed ahead of schedule. Airport Commissioner Anthony Peich, who provided a roast pig for the luncheon, told the gathering that the Chino Airport was in the process of becoming a first class general aviation airport. Chino Mayor Bob McCleod was quoted in the Chino Champion as telling the crowd; "We realize the impact of these additions to our airport more than any other city or surrounding county."

The Chino Judicial District was rapidly reaching a population of 40,000, the number necessary to gain a Municipal Court. Chino Police Chief Frank Meehan and I would drive around the Chino Valley looking for new housing foundations. For every new house foundation we located, we would add three more residents to our total. When we thought we had reached the magic 40,000 residents threshold, we presented our case to the Board of Supervisors. Chino Attorney Robley

Reher volunteered his services and we petitioned San Bernardino County to adhere to the law and replace our justice court with a municipal court.

At the next Board of Supervisor's meeting, I placed the petition on the agenda. After a meaningful discussion, the County Administrator, Robert Covington, was directed to verify the residential requirement and make a recommendation. I was generally pleased. A month later, Covington recommended Chino's justice court be added to the other municipal courts at the existing County building on Mountain Avenue at the I-10 Freeway in Ontario. I was not pleased.

The County Judges, the District Attorney, the Public Defender and the Sheriff enthusiastically supported Covington's recommendation. By this time, I was well versed in the art of persuasion. I was able to gain the support of Supervisors Dan Mikesell of Ontario and William Betterley from Apple Valley. Along with my support, a three-to-two vote converted the Chino Justice Court into the Chino Municipal Court and allowed it to remain in Chino.

Former Highway Patrolman, Ben Burrell, who was not an attorney, was the Chino Justice Court Judge at the time. He wasn't eligible to assume the duties of Judge of the Chino Municipal Court. He resigned his post as Chino Justice Court Judge prior to the changeover and became a Traffic Commissioner in the Ontario County Complex. I recommended to the Board of Supervisors the appointment of local Attorney Phillip Schaefer to replace Ben Burrell as Chino's Justice Court Judge. He was the only local attorney to seek the appointment and did so enthusiastically. The Board of Supervisors accepted my recommendation and Judge Schaefer served as Chino's Justice Court Judge until he became the first Municipal Court Judge of the Chino Municipal Court.

Fred Derbyshire, former Chino Chief of Police and retired California Highway Patrolman, was the Constable of the

Chino Justice Court before the conversion. He resigned shortly after Judge Burrell submitted his resignation. I asked Chief Frank Meehan if he had any recommendations for the Constable Derbyshire's replacement. Chief Meehan recommended one of his deputies, Bud Coppess, as an excellent candidate for Constable. With Bud agreeing to the shift in positions and the Board of Supervisors supporting my recommendation, Coppess became Constable of the Chino Justice Court. When the conversion to the Chino Municipal Court was complete, Bud assumed the position of Marshal, replacing the position of Constable.

As County Supervisor, I was able to provide the residents of the Los Serranos area of Chino Hills (at the time, much of Chino Hills was part of the unincorporated area of the County) the same opportunity I had provided the residents of Chino when I was Mayor by providing a "clean-up week." As the most western portion of the County, Los Serranos had been largely overlooked in making available municipal services to the residents. There were two empty lots located near Los Serranos Golf Course. I contacted the owners of the property and explained to them my plan. I wanted to establish a "clean-up week" in the area and use their property as a temporary trash collection site. I assured them that at the end of the week, all of the trash on their property would be removed and their property would be left as clean as it was before, if not cleaner. After three days of consideration, the owners agreed. County staff immediately distributed flyers announcing "clean-up week" throughout the area. Residents were informed they would be able to dump all forms of trash that could be loaded onto County dump trucks and hauled away to the Milliken Landfill throughout the entire week for free. After the week ended, front and back yards throughout the area were much improved. The program was a huge success.

One of my more difficult challenges as a County

Supervisor was my attempt to merge the County Marshals
Department with the County's Sheriffs Department. Common
sense dictated that a merger would eliminate duplication of
services and would create a more efficient operation.
Unfortunately, I couldn't initiate any support for the idea. The
Marshals and the Sheriffs were determined to protect their own
turfs and no one wanted to upset the apple cart. I suggested
that County officials meet with our then State Senator, William
Coombs, to discuss State legislation that would satisfy all stakeholders. Supervisor Mikesell, Municipal Court Judge Roy
Chapman, Sheriff Bland, the Marshal and I flew to Sacramento
to have a conference with him. Though there was a healthy
exchange of ideas, no one would budge enough to make any
merger possible.

It wasn't until I was a State Senator that I was able to
propose a bill. In 1987, a study was conducted indicating that
San Bernardino County could save between $700,000 and
$900,000 annually by consolidating court related services
between the Marshal's and the Sheriff's departments. Other
prominent counties throughout California had already saved
hundred of thousands of dollars by merging many functions of
the two departments. Twenty years later after I began the
effort, the time was right, the circumstances were good and I
was finally able to build a large enough consensus to pass
Senate Bill 242 in 1992. At times, the debate was intense, mostly on the county level. I can't help but consider how many millions of dollars San Bernardino County could have saved if the
consolidation of court related services between the Marshal's
and Sheriff's offices had been allowed when I first proposed it.
The negotiated bill ultimately provided County Judges with the
option of merging court related services performed by the
Marshal's Department into the Sheriff's Department or vice
versa. After so long a struggle, I felt great satisfaction in the
accomplishment and for the benefits finally derived.

It's also important to note that as Supervisor, I helped bring the Williamson Farm Land Protection Act to San Bernardino County. With the support of George Borba and other dairymen in the Chino Valley, we created the West End Agriculture Preserve. Prior to the enactment of Proposition 13, the County Assessors could, and at times did, increase property values to unreasonable heights, raising property tax bills immensely. Those who owned and farmed large parcels of land were being hit the hardest. Establishing the Agriculture Preserve protected farmers and dairymen from being taxed off their lands by setting lower property taxes on land used for agriculture. It also zoned the area for agriculture use only, preserving a significant rural heritage in the west end of the County. When I was elected State Senator, around 80% of the County's Agriculture Preserve was located in the Chino Valley.

In 2003 the Agriculture Preserve was decommissioned. The City of Chino annexed approximately 7,000 acres divided into two sub areas. Sub Area #1 covers approximately 1,600 acres with around 700 acres not developable due to being part of or close to the flood control basin area behind Prado Dam. Sub Area #2 covers approximately 5,400 acres with around 3,200 acres not developable for the same reason. The balance of the Preserve was annexed by the City of Ontario.

The Agriculture Preserve served its purpose and protected our agricultural and rural surroundings for a time. In the last decade, demand for suburban growth has increased dramatically, resulting in skyrocketing property values. Meanwhile, operational costs for farms and dairies have continued to rise while the selling prices of their products have been stagnant for decades. The landowners want to sell. The developers want to buy and the cities want to expand. It appears that the major stakeholders are all in agreement. However, I have my concerns.

It concerns me that those responsible for master

planning the decommissioned Preserve parcels appear to consider mostly warehousing and high-density residential developments. From a city government point of view, high-density housing usually costs more in public services than it generates in revenue.

Why not work to attract high-end industries, or perhaps a world-class medical research facility to study chronic diseases, such as Alzheimer's, cancer, heart disease, AIDS, etc.? Why not contact medical schools at the University of California, Stanford, USC, UCLA, etc. and propose a satellite facility for an outstanding school of medicine/research center? Of course, it wouldn't be that simple and it would require a lot of work and planning, but it could be done. With high-end industry comes high-end/lower-density housing and high-end retail, which combine to generate higher net income to the city. The proper balance of affordable housing is also important and should be included in the mix, along with parks and green space.

The current members of the Chino City Council ('05) appear to have the qualities required to change the ongoing stereotype that Chino is just a prison town. I understand a popular televison show recently fed into that negative stereotype. Chino City officials could petition the State of California to have CIM decommissioned and its property be put back on the tax roll and sold off to the right mix of developers under a progressive Chino Master Plan. As a State Senator, I organized a group of developers who were willing to purchase the California Institution for Men facilities and the Hemen G. Stark Youth Training School, covering nearly 2,500 acres. The State had originally purchased the property for around $650,000. Developers were willing to pay the estimated fair market value at the time of around $376 million (over $150,000 an acre). The money could then be used by the State to construct new correctional facilities in less densely populated areas. At the time, my proposal received tepid support from local officials and some resistance at the State level. I believe that with fervent local support and the right mix of developers, the State could be influenced to move its correctional facilities out of Chino.

From a regional perspective, I have watched as the West End of San Bernardino County has become more and more homogeneous, as we continue to experience unprecedented growth. Many of the challenges that Chino Valley faces are not much different than the challenges faced by its neighboring cities. These challenges, such as increased traffic, air quality, business development, affordable housing, etc. are more and more interrelated. I believe that the need for more regional planning and solutions continues to grow. Maybe it's time to consider a Regional Chamber of Commerce, along with greater utilization of joint powers in regional development. Certainly we need to do more regional planning. As a region, we are dependent on the same highways, airport, air, etc. Working together regionally, just makes more and more sense.

On February 27, 2003, at a dinner held at the Red Hill Country Club, former Ontario Mayor and Chairman of the San Bernardino County Board of Supervisors, Daniel Mikesell, was honored with the West End Public Service Award. He was the award's first recipient. He was 92 years old. I attended and was proud to say without any contradiction that Dan's public service to the County's West End communities was without comparison. Sam Crowe, Master of Ceremonies for the occasion, put it very succinctly when he said, "Many people receiving invitations to tonight's dinner could be placed into two categories: The ones who probably wondered, 'Who the hell is Dan Mikesell and those who probably wondered, 'Why did it take so long?'" Although I had served on the Chino School Board, on the Chino City Council and as Chino's First Elected Mayor, before being elected to the San Bernardino County Board of Supervisors, I can honestly say that Dan was a great local government mentor for me.

CHAPTER SEVEN

THE CALL TO HIGHER OFFICE

In 1972, a new Congressional District was formed. It included the Chino Valley. It was named the 38th Congressional District. Many friends and supporters encouraged me to run for the open seat. I listened and responded. I entered the race to represent the newly created District, encompassing parts of San Bernardino and Riverside Counties. There were four Democratic candidates in the Primary. They were David Tunno from Riverside, a former aide to Senator John Tunney; former Monterey Park Congressman George E. Brown; a wealthy young attorney, Terry Goggin; and Ruben S. Ayala, the Chairman of the San Bernardino County Board of Supervisors. George Brown and Terry Goggin moved into the Congressional District just to run for this new Congressional seat. It was a bitter Primary election. Ultimately, I narrowly lost to Congressman George Brown, who beat me in Riverside County. He went on to win the General Election against Ontario Mayor Howard Snider, a Republican.

    Cesar Chavez, the well-known founder of the National Farm Workers Association, which later became the United Farm Workers, came out in support of George Brown. After the election, at a rally at Redlands University, Chavez told students that I had been active in Imperial County attempting to break a farm workers strike. I read the account in the

93

newspaper and couldn't believe what I was reading. It just was-
n't true. I was a Supervisor of San Bernardino County. I didn't
have anything to do with Imperial County. After many calls to
Cesar Chavez's office, I was finally able to talk to him and clarify what I considered to be a complete falsehood. We met at a
restaurant in the City of San Bernardino and Cesar Chavez personally assured me that he would straighten things out. With
television cameras and reporters waiting outside, Cesar then
told the press that we had had "our differences, but we had ...
worked them out." That was it. Unfortunately, that was the
closest I ever got to an apology or to a correction to the story.
Needless to say, I was very disappointed.

Although the Democratic Congressional Primary
involved four important candidates, the battle was fought mostly between Congressman Brown and myself. In retrospect, I
think my support of the County Counsel's legal opinion refus-
ing to provide welfare benefits to striking steelworkers at Kaiser
Steel in Fontana most likely cost me many votes.

I also supported our sons and daughters who were
ordered by our Federal Government to fight in Vietnam. An
incident that occurred on the University of California at
Riverside campus best illustrates what I was up against during
the Congressional Primary campaign. I was speaking before
students at U.C. Riverside, where former Congressman George
Brown had spoken the day before. Apparently, most of the
issues the Congressman supported, I opposed. Brown was for
giving blanket amnesty to any and all who fled our country to
Canada to avoid the draft. I felt that each case should be
judged on its own merits. I thought that those who warranted
being pardoned should be given amnesty. However, those who
did not deserve it, should not receive it. No Blanket Amnesty!
Brown told the students that he was for legalizing the general
use of marijuana. I took the position that until a medical finding determined that the use of marijuana was not harmful, I

would not support it as a non-prescription drug.

Brown was for women's choice in abortion matters. I supported legalizing abortion only in cases where the mother's life was in danger or in the case of rape or incest.

I further emphasized that I supported our young men and women fighting in Vietnam and favored their receiving the very best resources to do their job.

When I concluded my remarks, I inquired if there were any questions. No one responded. I was met only with blank stares from the students. Finally, after what seemed like an eternity, a student with extremely long hair approached the microphone. I was so relieved to have someone ask a question that I mistook the student for a young woman. Too quickly, I inquired, "Yes, Ma'am, do you have a question?" The crowd snickered. The student replied very loudly and clearly, confirming his male gender, "Yes, Sir, I do have a question. Who else is running?"

October 25, 1973 was a hot day in Redding, California. As President of the Southern California Regional Association of County Supervisors, I was attending a conference of the County Supervisors Association of California (CSAC) at the Red Lion Inn. Fellow Supervisor William (Bill) Betterley and N. J. (Rusty) Rustin, Vice President of the Owl Asphalt Company, had just joined Irene and me for lunch in the lounge. During our meal, I was paged over the Inn's public address system. I excused myself and walked over to the lobby desk to answer the call. It was my secretary, Wilma (Willie) Silva. She wanted to inform me that some very interesting political activity was taking place in my County District. Our State Senator, Republican William Coombs, had just announced his resignation from the Senate and, almost simultaneously, Republican Assemblyman Jerry Lewis had announced his candidacy for the State Senate Seat. Willie excitedly told me that people had already called my office urging me to seek the now open

Senate Seat.

I remembered that Senator Coombs had told me that he was hoping to be appointed to the Superior Court in the County of San Bernardino. He had mentioned he was disappointed that he had not heard from Governor Ronald Reagan in regards to his request. The announcement of his resignation should not have been a great surprise to me, but it was. It turned out that Senator Coombs had accepted a position with the President Nixon's Administration in Washington, D.C.

After my conversation with Willie, I remember staying by the phone for a few moments as all kinds of thoughts spiraled through my mind. When I relayed the exciting news to Irene and our lunch companions, Rusty Rustin reached into his pocket and handed me a half dollar. He declared, "This is the first contribution to the Ayala for Senate Campaign." I still have that half dollar and will always treasure it.

After the conference was over, Irene and I drove from Redding to Eureka for a short visit with my brother Maury and his wife Kay. We then flew to Los Angeles where a member of my staff told us that Assemblyman Jerry Lewis was already off and running in pursuit of the Senate Seat. Since there were now 19 Republicans in the State Senate and 20 Democrats, a Republican win would make it even. Republican Lieutenant-Governor Ed Reineke could break any ties in favor of the Republicans, giving them control of the California State Senate. This was also the first partisan race in the nation since the Watergate scandal had hit Washington, D.C.

After discussing the Senate race with Irene, other family members and supporters from throughout my County District, I called a press conference to announce my candidacy for the California State Senate. No one seemed to be surprised. The interest in the race at the local, state and national levels, was intense right from the beginning.

Mike Valles, San Bernardino native and Assemblyman

John Quimby's Chief of Staff, took a leave of absence to manage my campaign. Mike was highly regarded as a political strategist, both in San Bernardino and Sacramento.

The Senate's open seat also attracted the interest of Democrat Ralph Carter, a Rialto Councilman, and Republican Robert Allenthrop, a Big Bear Lake businessman. Assemblyman Lewis, a San Bernardino native and a very popular officeholder, was considered the frontrunner for the Primary Election, due to his head start.

The 20th Senate District encompassed the entire County of San Bernardino, excluding Redlands. Among the candidates, the Primary Election appeared to be somewhat relaxed. We were like boxers, feeling each other out in the early rounds of a fight. Our camp was not convinced that any candidate, even the frontrunner, could acquire a majority of the votes and outright win the Senate seat in the Primary Election.

The Primary Election for the California State Senate 20th District seat was held on December 15, 1973, just days before Christmas. Our objective was to come in first in the Primary and use the momentum to carry us forward into the General Election.

The Lewis people thought differently. In campaign spending, they went for broke right from the beginning. They outspent us over three-to-one in the Primary Election. As a result, Assemblyman Jerry Lewis captured 49.1 percent of the Primary Election vote. If Assemblyman Lewis had received just 1 percent more of the vote, he would have won the Senate Seat outright, without having to continue on to the General Election.

Coming in at a close second, I still had a chance to win the Senate seat in the upcoming General Election. Our analysis of the results of the Primary Election indicated that only 26 percent of eligible voters went to the polls. Our mission for the General Election was clear. We had to galvanize our supporters and get them out to vote. Just after the Primary Election, during Christmastime, Jerry sent me a lovely bouquet of roses. The challenge was on. I don't believe I can find words to describe the excitement and enthusiasm of the "Ayala for Senate" supporters. They worked extremely hard and effectively up to and during the General Election on January 15, 1974, just one month following the Primary Election.

Jerry Lewis and I debated over local radio stations and local cable television. It appeared that everywhere I spoke, Jerry had been there or was scheduled to make an appearance. He even suggested that he would be happy to fly down from Sacramento and debate me on a daily basis if I agreed. In political campaigns, frontrunners normally don't go around challenging their opponents to debates. We readily surmised that his surveys of the race showed that I was closing in on his initial lead. It was important to me that we only debated as often as I felt was advantageous to me to deliver my message.

Between February 1 and February 15 of 1972, Kaiser Steel workers had gone on strike at the Fontana Mill. Some of the steel workers had applied for Welfare benefits during my tenure as Chairman of the San Bernardino County Board of Supervisors. Our County Counsel, Stan Herlick, expressed his legal opinion to the Board that the Steel Mill Workers were not eligible for Welfare benefits because they had gone on strike over fringe benefits and not over wages. He concluded that the only workers at the mill eligible for welfare benefits, assuming they met the other general qualifications, would be the secretarial staff. The Steel Workers' Union was up in arms about Herlick's opinion. I determined that until the Board was given a different opinion from a higher legal authority that I would adopt the same position.

Before the General Election, Jerry and I were debating over San Bernardino Community College Cable TV and taking questions from the viewers. I don't know whether it was a plant by the Lewis Camp or not, but one caller sounded very irate. She was extremely upset with me over the fact that I had refused to authorize welfare benefits for the steelworkers who were on strike. She wanted to know what kind of a Democrat I was. Before I could respond, Jerry jumped in and stated that sometimes the laws ought to be bent a little in the interest of our citizens. He went on to say that if he had been asked about the issue at the time, he would have supported the steel-workers. My response was immediate and direct. I said that, "Bending the law was exactly what happened in Washington, D.C. to his Republican colleagues. They thought they were above the law. So if you want someone to represent you who will obey the laws of the land, I am that person. If you want someone who will bend the laws a little, when he finds it con-venient, then Mr. Lewis is your man."

This exchange probably won me the debate and, more importantly, many undecided voters. On the Sunday evening before Election Day, Republicans presented us with a big break. Governor Ronald Reagan put on a fundraiser for Jerry at the Governor's Mansion. Attending were the high-powered Sacramento lobbyists, including oil, insurance, banking and real estate interests. No one would know prior to the election who attended, because disclosure would not be required to be reported to the Fair Political Practice Commission until after Election Day. We capitalized on this hush-hush fundraiser. We ran a full-page advertisement in the next morning's edition of the San Bernardino Sun. It included an enlarged photograph of the invitation to the dinner and pointedly associated Jerry Lewis with out-of-county big money, strongly declaring, "San Bernardino County was not for sale." We also made it clear that the road back from Watergate would begin in San Bernardino County with Ayala as State Senator.

Election Day was a beehive in San Bernardino. Busloads of supporters for both candidates arrived early and were dispersed to assigned areas. As my supporters arrived, I would board the buses, shake hands and thank them for their help on Election Day. Each was given a lunch box with Kentucky Fried Chicken and a soft drink. Their goal was to "GET OUT THE VOTE!"

Most of these folks returned to our headquarters after the polls closed. State and national political leaders, from both sides of the aisle, helped get out the vote. Republican Congressman Vic Vasey and State Controller Houston Flournoy were seen walking precincts for Jerry. Former Governor Pat Brown, U.S. Senators Alan Cranston and John V. Tunney and Congressmen Phil and John Burton were among my supporters. Senate pro-tem Jim Mills and State Senator George Zenovich and their staffs, who had taken a leave of absence, were also in San Bernardino helping our cause.

Our main headquarters was located in a large commercial building on Mt. Vernon Street in San Bernardino. As the polls closed, our get-out-the vote volunteers began to return to headquarters. By 8 p.m., the Ayala for Senate Headquarters was wall-to-wall with our supporters. Excitement, with the anticipation of victory, was evident. Irene, our three sons and I mingled throughout the crowd, despite the private room set aside by our committee for us to watch the returns.

By 9 p.m., the results were coming in at a rapid pace and we could see a slight gain with each report. A favorable trend was emerging. By 11:30 p.m., I had forged ahead by a fairly good margin. Then a little after midnight, although not all the votes had been counted, Mike Valles, who was manning the phones, came up to me with a smile and told me Jerry was calling. Jerry offered his congratulations and told me that he and his wife were on their way to my headquarters to personally and publicly congratulate me. I tried to dissuade him from coming over. There were so many people inside the building that it would be difficult to get in. Even the street in front of the building was crowded with supporters. I thanked Jerry and expressed my best wishes. I told him I would relay his message to the crowd. He insisted on coming over, anyway.

I then went over to the public address unit and informed the huge crowd that Assemblyman Lewis had just called and conceded the election. People inside the building and out in the street erupted in cheers. I was finally able to quiet them long enough to tell them Assemblyman Lewis and his wife were on their way over to personally congratulate us. I also indicated to them that it takes a lot of courage for them to do so. I said we should show our class by giving them the respect they deserved.

Jerry and his wife came over just as they said they would. We shook hands and hugged in front of supporters. An extremely hard fought political campaign was over. With all 275 precincts reporting and all votes tallied, I had received 45,075 votes or 54.1% of the electorate. Assemblyman Jerry Lewis claimed 38,325, or 45.9%.

Political analysts had a field day telling us why Ayala had won and Lewis had lost. Some pointed the finger at President Nixon and the Watergate scandal. Others blamed all that big out-of-county money coming into the Lewis Campaign Committee from the Sacramento lobbyists in the closing days of the Election. They had a difficult time explaining how we were able to sweep 11 out of 14 cities in the county. We failed, by small margins, to carry Upland, Victorville and Adelanto. John L. Harmer, Chairman of the State Senate Republican Caucus, was quoted as saying the day after the election, "It was a great mistake for the GOP Legislative candidates to raise campaign funds outside their districts in the post-Watergate era."

I can say without fear of contradiction that Jerry Lewis was the toughest, most sophisticated and competitive political opponent I faced in all of my 43 years of elective office.

Nevertheless, he has always impressed me as being a classy individual whom I respect and genuinely like. Today, Jerry is a powerful member of the United States Congress and Chairman of the House Appropriations Committee. He recently celebrated his 25th anniversary as a member of the United States Congress. I can't help but consider how our lives would have been had the results of our election been different. I think we both are satisfied with the way things turned out.

After the Election, during one of my early legislative efforts as a State Senator, I asked Assemblyman Lewis if he would carry one of my bills through the Assembly. Jerry agreed and gave an outstanding presentation on the Assembly floor on behalf of the bill's passage. As a result, my bill easily obtained the necessary votes for passage. However, I was surprised to find out that the final vote count indicated that Jerry had actually voted against my bill, despite his favorable presentation. When the press found out, they asked Jerry to explain his "no" vote after advocating the bill's passage so effectively. He merely responded that he hadn't quite convinced himself to vote for it.

I'm not sure it's possible to organize and promote a perfect political campaign, but the "Ayala for Senate" campaign of January 1974 came close to it. Thanks to my family, friends and thousands of loyal and hard working supporters, our Senate Campaign was a disciplined effort that reached its peak at the most appropriate time - on Election Day.

On January 23, 1974, a large number of our area citizens, including Dad and Irene's mother, traveled to Sacramento to witness my taking the oath of office as California's newest State Senator. For my Dad and mother-in-law, it was their first time on an airplane. It was truly a momentous occasion for all of us.

That evening we celebrated by attending several parties held in my honor. After making several appearances, my family

and I had dinner by ourselves. I can't possibly express how
meaningful it was for me to be with my family on such a significant occasion in my life. I am so grateful to my family and
friends for all they have done to support me throughout the
years. They went on to help me win re-election for 6 more
terms, just 23 days shy of 25 years in total, until newly set term
limits ended my career in the California State Senate on
December 31, 1998.

"Up From Second Street"   Ruben S. Ayala

CHAPTER EIGHT

WATER! A PRECIOUS RESOURCE

The morning after I was sworn in as the newest member of the California State Senate, the Sacramento press corps greeted me at my new office. I was bombarded with a multitude of questions. I remember one reporter asked me whether I viewed my election as an opportunity to become a spokesman in the California Legislature for the Mexican-American community. One newspaper had declared me as "... the first authentic Mexican-American State Senator California has ever had." I responded that I was very proud of my heritage, but I viewed the election as an opportunity to speak for all of my constituents, regardless of their ethnicity.

Another reporter, obviously knowing of my early beginnings in the Chino Barrio, asked me if I had ever been a member of a gang. I and most of my buddies growing up were involved in athletics. We never even considered the possibility of joining a gang. My Dad would have clobbered me. Initially, I was somewhat offended by the implication. I thought about answering by asking the reporter if he had ever belonged to a gang. Instead, I restrained myself and was about to respond that I had never belonged to a gang when it occurred to me that I had indeed once been a member of a gang. So, I replied that, yes, I had once belonged to a gang. The reporter hastily scribbled away on his pad as if he had just discovered a big story. Nearly interrupting, he rushed to ask, "What was the name of the gang?" I paused to answer as the reporter

105

anxiously waited with pen in hand. "Well," I slowly replied, "You may have heard of us. I belonged to the United States Marines. Some gang!" I said. The reporter's grip on his pen immediately relaxed.

As a new State Senator, there were my more liberal colleagues who made it very clear that they viewed my more conservative record with suspicion. Their opinion certainly was not the majority. Senator Ken Maddy from the Fresno area was quoted, "Ruben will give some good moderate leadership."

I remember a few days later, I received a call from Governor Ronald Reagan, asking me to come to his office for a chat. San Bernardino County Supervisor Dennis Hansberger happened to be in my office at the time, so I invited him to join me. We shared an enjoyable conversation with the Governor. In my 25 years as a State Senator, I served with Governors Ronald Reagan, Jerry Brown, George Deukmejian and Pete Wilson. Of the four, I believe Governor Reagan was the most amiable.

As a freshman legislator, I was surprised and delighted to be named to the committees on Revenue and Taxation, Local Government, Agriculture and Water Resources, and Natural Resources and Wildlife. Sometime later, I was transferred to the Transportation Committee in place of the Natural Resources and Wildlife Committee.

My initial election to the Senate was only to complete the time left in Senator Coombs' term. I had to campaign again that following November, only 11 months after the Special Election. I ran unapposed in the Primary and in the General, I ran against a Republican attorney with much less charisma and political appeal than Jerry Lewis. I won by a significant margin. Counting the Primaries, we ran four campaigns for four different elections in just 11 months to be able to serve just one complete four year term in the State Senate. It seemed at the time that I must have set some kind of record.

One of the first rudimentary displays of vigorous partisan politics I witnessed as a California State Senator was my first exposure to the State Fiscal Budget. It was presented for approval at one of my first Senate meetings. I recall the Senators being summoned through the public address system to convene in the Senate Chambers. The tone was one of urgency. Arriving at our desks on the Senate floor, we each found neatly placed on our desks four huge volumes making up the proposed 1974-1975 Fiscal Budget for the State of California.

Having had years of experience with school, city and county budgets, I wasn't cherishing the idea of sitting at my desk and gazing for the first time at this overwhelming amount of material so important to all Californians. I was expecting to have the opportunity to review at least some of the documents before the discussion and voting began. Nevertheless, the debate began almost immediately.

Senator Randy Collier (D) from Yreka, the Chairman of the Senate Finance and Budget Committee, began by briefly explaining the major contents of the budget. I tried to appear as astute as possible as I listened with much interest to both sides of the aisle passionately argue. At times, the debate became sharply unpleasant and emotional. The debate ricocheted from one end of the ideological spectrum to the other with negative personal characterizations sprinkled in between. The partisan fervor led me to consider what I believed then and what I believe now - that state legislators have the responsibility to work through the challenges facing our state as objectively as possible without regard to politics, emotions or prejudices. After listening to much of the debate, I was leaning to not voting for the proposed budget bill.

About that time, Senate Minority Floor Leader George Deukmejian (R) stood and asked Senator Collier to explain what the language contained in a certain volume, page and line number meant. Senator Deukmejian indicated that he didn't understand the intent of the wording. Senator Collier sharply responded that the Senator should not expect to understand the wording because he was not a member of the Senate Finance and Budget Committee. Many members shook their heads in disbelief at the implications of Senator Collier's autocratic response. I thought to myself, "Does that mean that I should never expect to understand a budget that I am asked to vote for on behalf of my constituents unless I become a member of the Senate Finance and Budget Committee?"

Debate soon came to a close and Senator Collier made the final arguments in support of the budget. It was time for a roll call vote. One by one we voted. By then I knew where I stood. My vote was the first "No" vote recorded. The initial roll call failed to achieve enough support. After several more roll call votes the bill failed to garner enough support and was declared "dead."

Prior to the final declaration of the bill's failure by Senate Pro Tem Mills, Senator Collier arose from his seat and marched over to my desk with his face red with rage. In front of others, he loudly scolded me, "Young man, you are new here. You are to be seen and not heard!"

Other Democratic leaders more politely asked me to reconsider. I could not and respectfully explained my reasons. I wasn't going to vote for something that I hadn't had enough time to review and whose authors were unwilling to answer simple questions concerning its contents. Senator Claire Berryhill also visited my desk and told me, "When I heard you vote 'No' on that bill, I said to myself that if a freshman Senator can say 'No' to Senator Collier with all of his influence then so can I." Claire Berryhill went on to become the Director of the California Department of Food and Agriculture during Governor Deukmejian's administration.

A second budget conference was scheduled for a future

date. Amendments were made to accommodate significant differences and the second bill passed with my "Aye" vote. From that point on, I don't think my "Aye" vote was ever taken for granted by the leadership of the party or the Senate.

Two years into my first term, Senator Howard Way, Chairman of the Agriculture and Water Resources Committee, decided against running for re-election. In those days, freshman Senate Legislators weren't usually appointed to chair a committee. They had to earn such positions of responsibility and it usually took more than one term in office, assuming they continued to win re-election. Due to term limits, this is not the case anymore.

I imagine I was chosen because of the substantial agricultural activity in my Senate District and perhaps my 20 years experience as an elected local government official was taken into consideration, also. In any case, Senate President Pro-Tem James Mills and the Senate Rules Committee made an exception in naming me the Chairman of the Water Resources Committee. I chaired the Committee for eighteen years. I resigned the Chairmanship when Senate Pro-Tem David Roberti appointed me to the highly regarded and influential Senate Rules Committee.

I retained my Senate Water Consultant, Steve Macola. Steve was an engineer and, in my opinion, one of the leading experts regarding California water issues. At times, Steve had a problem getting along with folks in the water industry, but that did not take away from his extensive and comprehensive knowledge of California's immense water conflicts and challenges.

To initiate my tenure as the Water Resources Chairman, Steve and I sat down and went over all of the State's water issues that should be brought before the Committee, including plans that had been on a shelf for many years. We were determined to address California's ongoing challenge with its most precious resource, water.

"Up From Second Street"   Ruben S. Ayala

Without a continual healthy water supply, California cannot continue to prosper as it has over the last decades. Arguably, water is California's most precious resource. With its population continually increasing, California cannot afford to ignore its water issues or procrastinate implementing programs to mitigate the increasing challenge. Because water is a limited resource, all of the stakeholders must be willing to compromise.

As we worked through many different mitigating programs, the "Peripheral Canal" project showed up on our radar screen. I was immediately intrigued and fascinated with the idea of moving surplus water from one area of abundance to the more needy arid sectors of California, with protections to the areas of origin and the environment.

Of course, I was not the first to concern myself with California's water issues. On July 5, 1956, the California State Legislature created the State Department of Waters Resources. Its purpose was to plan and guide the State's water resources into the future. In 1957, the Department completed the California Water Plan. It contained preliminary plans for developing all of the State's water resources to meet California's future water needs. It included a system of reservoirs, aqueducts and pumping plants that would transfer water from areas of surplus in the northern part of the State to the water-deficient south. The California State Water Project (SWP) would be a tremendous undertaking. I became an avid student of the project.

Furthermore, in 1959, the Legislature authorized the Burns-Porter Act. It provided initial funding of $1.75 billion in general obligation bonds. In 1960, California voters approved the measure. The Burns-Porter Act did not specify or name the transfer facilities to be constructed. There were several surveys done to determine the most efficient system of transport. Each clearly indicated that constructing a 42-mile peripheral canal, bypassing the Delta to the east, was by far the most desirable. This Peripheral Canal would be the most efficient and effective method to protect the area of origin, the native marine life and the rest of the environment.

State projections indicated that by the year 2020, almost 50 million people would live in California (Note: the 2000 U.S. Census population for California was 34 million, up by 4.2 million from the 1990 U.S. Census, which was up by 6 million from the 1980 U.S. Census). It was clear to me that more water would be needed to meet growing urban and industrial demands, sustain agriculture production and still maintain stream flows for fish, recreation, water quality, salinity control and navigation.

After a thorough review of the surveys and testimonials on record, I introduced SB (Senate Bill) 346 as a spot bill in support of the construction of the Peripheral Canal. A spot bill is a bill with a number assigned to it, but the language only includes those sections of the law that the bill will address. The bill is then amended to indicate specifically what an author has in mind before it's assigned to the proper committee for hearing. Sometimes the author may have public hearings on his or her own spot bill. This is usually done to make certain that with input from interested parties, the bill is in its best form for committee hearings.

Steve and I had many discussions with members of the water and farming communities and the environmentalists, before our first hearing in the Agriculture and Water Resources Committee. We wanted to properly prep the wheel. But, as soon as I amended SB 346 to call for the construction of the Peripheral Canal on the east boundary of the Delta, the phone calls and nasty letters from our northern kin came pouring in. As the process developed, some got ugly.

SB 346 required the approval of at least two-thirds of the members of both houses of the State legislature, the Senate and the Assembly. After considerable difficulty, we managed to get approval from the Senate. On the Assembly Water Committee, SB 346 was amended against my preference. The amended bill was given passage on the Assembly floor and returned to the Senate for concurrence on the Assembly amendments. However, SB 346, as amended in the Assembly, could not get the two-thirds majority vote on the Senate floor. By the time I could muster the necessary votes, the 1977-1978 Senate Session had ended.

Early in the 1979-1980 Legislation Session, I introduced SB 200. The new bill had a few modifications from SB 346. One modification changed the number of votes required for passage. While SB 346 needed at least two-thirds support from both houses, SB 200 needed only a simple majority. The difference is that a bill receiving two-thirds support and the Governor's signature becomes law the same day the Governor signs it. A bill receiving a simple majority of the votes and signed by the Governor becomes law the following January 1st. I thought with a simple majority requirement, we would avoid some of the previous setbacks. Unfortunately, SB 200 immediately attracted a new wave of opposition.

During the same legislative session and in response to my proposed SB 200, Assemblyman Larry Kapiloff of San Diego introduced Assembly Constitutional Amendment 90 (ACA90) that directly affected the success of SB 200. ACA 90, in part, placed all of northern California's rivers under the Wild Rivers and Scenic Act. Under Kapiloff's ACA, this would only occur if SB 200 became law. In other words, his legislation would only go into effect if SB 200 passed. Governor Jerry Brown signed the Kapiloff Legislation and because it was a constitutional amendment, it was presented to voters as Proposition 8 on the November 1980 ballot. It passed with 53.3% of the votes. The end result was that if SB 200 became law, northern California's rivers would be frozen under the Wild

Rivers and Scenic Act. ACA 90 put so many obstacles in place that it was not reasonable to expect that any waterways in northern California could be developed or diverted for any purposes if SB 200 passed.

The "environmentalists" approved of Kapiloff's proposed constitutional amendment, but still ferociously opposed SB 200. Kapiloff's legislation turned off many of the farming community, especially agriculture business interests. The farmers believed if Kapiloff's ACA was triggered by SB 200, then they would lose too many of their developing and diversion rights. The environmentalists felt they were not getting very much from the Kapiloff Legislation and wanted even more protection. In a surprising coalition, farmers and environmentalists joined forces to help kill passage of SB 200.

Due to the simple majority requirement for passage of SB 200, it cleared both houses in a relatively short period of time. Governor Jerry Brown finally signed SB 200 in his Los Angeles Office. Under glaring television lights, my most important and much debated piece of legislation received the signature of the Governor. Governor Brown was then running against Pete Wilson from San Diego for U.S. Senator. To the consternation of many of the Peripheral Canal supporters, he never again raised his voice in favor of the water transfer facility again.

The bill was scheduled to become law on January 1, 1983. Unfortunately, the delayed effective date gave the environmentalists the time they needed to gather signatures to petition its repeal through the initiative process. Enough signatures were obtained to place the matter directly before voters at the November 1982 General Election. Plenty of money and hoopla were injected into the campaign by both sides of the issue. At the end of the day, those against the water transfer facility ran a much better campaign than those who supported it. Sixty-two percent of voters voted against Proposition 9 titled, "WATER FACILITIES INCLUDING A PERIPHERAL CANAL." SB 200 was taken off the books before it became law by the referendum vote of the people and the Peripheral Canal proposal was defeated once again.

It's difficult to explain why a piece of legislation, designed to better serve and enhance water supplies for southern and central California into the future, while protecting northern California water supplies and environment, would go down to defeat by popular vote. The fact is that two-thirds of California's population lives south of the Tehachapi Mountains. One third of our population resides from the Tehachapis to the Oregon border. SB 200 had built-in protection for the area of origin, the fisheries and the environment, while assuring an increased water supply to southern and central California. According to the water experts, who we depended on for guidance and direction, the Peripheral Canal was by far the best available solution to meet the State of California's growing water demand.

In my judgment, the Peripheral Canal should be built someday, perhaps under a different label. In order to reduce or eliminate future critical shortages in the southern and central portions of our State, I believe we must identify a facility that will allow the legal transfer of potable water from areas of abundance to areas of need. We can build that facility with the State Water Project Bond, passed by the California voters in 1960. That transfer facility must protect the areas of origin as required by existing law. In the meantime, we must continue to seek new ways to reduce our water consumption, and where possible, identify all legitimate alternative sources. I'm afraid, like so many things in government, we will only act when a crisis situation is upon us instead of properly preparing for the challenges we know are coming.

Water conservation, reuse, recycling and desalination must be strongly encouraged and supported. We must pursue more government and industry partnerships to preserve water. As an example, some soda plants in India provide treated wastewater free-of-charge to local farmers. In Pennsylvania, a Gatorade plant has provided nutrient rich wastewater to farmers to use in growing animal feed. We must continue to develop creative ways to reduce our water usage and utilize our wastewater to meet our needs.

It is difficult to comprehend the close-mindedness of some of our northern California citizens and their continual objection to allow surplus water from the North to flow south to the more arid areas of our state. Existing law completely protects the area of origin. The area of origin is always guaranteed whatever water it needs before a surplus can be diverted. Under State law, not one drop of water can be transferred until all needs of the area of origin have been met. The Peripheral Canal project would not change those protections at all. Some of our northern Californians blindly ignore those protections. They make the outrageous claim that the rest of California is out to deprive the North of its water.

Interestingly enough, the same folks take the opposite position when it comes to sharing revenues derived from Tide-Land Oil drilling. The last time I looked there wasn't a single offshore drilling rig north of Santa Barbara. Yet, a large portion of State revenues that flow from offshore drilling in the southern part of our State are used to finance, in part, State water projects and secondary education facilities in the North. The decision of how the money is spent is not based on geography, but on where the greatest need lies in the State, as it should be. There is no mention by anyone about protecting the area of origin in this case.

One of my local accomplishments began with Senate Bill (SB) 1971. In May of 1974, at the urging of Ray Furguson, the General Manager of the then Chino Basin Municipal Water District (CBMWB), with expertise in the water district's potable water issues, I introduced SB 1971. Over the years, Chino Basin's water users had been dangerously overdrafting the underground aquifer. Since water users had never been monitored or regulated for pumping water out of the Basin, scientific data and legal water rights had to be established. SB 1971 was designed to enable the where-with-all for this much needed ratification. Besides creating a "Water Master" for the Basin, it permitted the local water district to levy a pump tax of up to $2 an acre foot of water pumped out of the Basin to fund the monitoring and regulation of the Basin's water supply to assure a consistent supply of healthy local water.

Several local public hearings were held on the matter. Some of my dairy friends objected to the tax citing that politicians seldom remove a tax once imposed even when the need for the tax is no longer necessary. In response to their concerns, I amended the bill to read that once $250,000 had been generated or by the end of fiscal year 1975-1976, the tax would be lifted. Once that criteria was met, the pump tax became history.

Another local accomplishment, in terms of potable water delivery, was working with the newly created Water Facilities Agency in the early 1980's. The W.F.A., as it was otherwise known, was made up of the west-end cities of San Bernardino county. They were planning to build a water filtration plant on the Metropolitan District line, which runs along the Foothills to the "Met" Filtration Plant in La Verne. The proposed filtration plant was crucial because with it, the west-end cities would be able to tap into the supply of water flowing south into the region from northern California via the California Aqueduct (Governor Pat Brown's widely acclaimed water project).

Mayor Bob Ellingwood of the City of Ontario and Chairman of the W.F.A. called me for help to bond the project. "Bonding the project" would allow the W.F.A. to borrow the

116

money necessary to finance the project by selling certificates of debt (bonds) with set terms and guarantees for repayment. The State of California had previously authorized cities to band together to bond just about any public works project except water projects. The W.F.A. needed me to introduce enabling legislation allowing bonding for their specific water project. Time was of the essence, as the Federal Government was considering changing the bonding procedures which could have dramatically set back the project.

I readily agreed to assist the W.F.A., but the deadline for introducing new bills that year had already passed. I would have to find a bill already in the "pipeline," preferably a Senate Bill that the author had decided not to move any further and that was germane to the W.F.A.'s needs. With the author's consent of such a bill, the Senate Rules Committee could assign the bill to me.

My staff analyzed all of the other Senators' bills to find an appropriate vehicle, but without success. Mayor Ellingwood soon called back and I had to give him the bad news. However, as we were talking, it occurred to me that my staff had not researched my inventory of water related bills. We were delighted when we discovered a bill that I had already introduced that I could amend to accommodate the needs of the W.F.A. The bill passed and became law, allowing the W.F.A. to sell the necessary bonds to construct the water filtration plant.

Today, the water filtration plant is located in Upland, on N. Benson Avenue and supplies over 60 million gallons a day of water from northern California to all of the west-end cities of San Bernardino County, except Rancho Cucamonga. The water filtration plant is called, "Agua de Lejos," translated to mean, "Water From Afar." For almost two decades now, the only supply of northern California water to the west-end of San Bernardino County has been filtered through this facility.

As Chairman of the Senate Agriculture and Water

Resources Committee, I was fortunate to have been the guest of countries experiencing shortages of water suitable for human consumption. The Peripheral Canal legislation drew wide interest. Irene and I accepted invitations from Israel on three separate occasions. We also accepted invitations to visit Taiwan, Mexico, Australia, New Zealand, the Union of Soviet Socialist Republics and Finland. We also enjoyed visiting Japan, Denmark and England. I was appointed by both Governors Jerry Brown and George Deukmejian to serve as the representative from California on the Western States Water Council, which dealt with regional water issues. Its members came from states ranging from Texas to Alaska and Hawaii. As the California representative, I presented papers at meetings in Hawaii, Alaska and Jackson Hole, Wyoming. I was also honored in 1985 as the "Legislator of the Year" by the Association of Water Agencies and by the San Bernardino-Riverside Branch of the American Public Works Association for my work on the Peripheral Canal and other water related legislation.

CHAPTER NINE

FROM VISION TO REALITY

THE CALIFORNIA CONSERVATION CORPS

Franklin D. Roosevelt, our 32nd President, took office in 1933 in the midst of the Great Depression. The nation was facing an unprecedented retreating economy with dangerously rising unemployment. President Roosevelt initiated his Presidency by taking a number of important steps to provide relief to millions of suffering Americans. Almost immediately, he established a historic number and variety of government programs known as Roosevelt's "New Deal." One of his favorite programs was the creation of the Civilian Conservation Corps (CCC). Of the program, President Roosevelt said, "I propose to create a Civilian Conservation Corps to be used in simple work, not interfering with normal employment, and confining itself to forestry, the prevention of soil erosion, flood control and similar projects. More important, however, than the material gains, will be the moral and spiritual value of such work."

The Civilian Conservation Corps was a program established to train and employ our nation's unemployed and unmarried young men between the ages of 18 and 25. President Roosevelt signed the CCC into existence by signing U.S. Senate Bill 5.598 on March 31, 1933. The CCC recruits developed and conserved natural resources through reforestation (planting trees), restoration of National and State parks, flood control projects and fire protection. In all, 2.5 million young men and 8,500 young women would participate in and benefit from the program. Provided room and board in conservation camps run by the Army, these young workers earned $1 a day while working to conserve our nation's natural resources. As U.S. involvement in World War II expanded, the need for the CCC was dominated by the war effort. Congress terminated the program in 1942.

Prior to the beginning of the 1976 Legislative Session, I mailed constituents a newsletter indicating my intent to introduce legislation to establish a program pattterned after the Prersident Roosevelt's Civilian Conservation Corps. I was concerned that too many of our young adults were drifting away from formal education and discipline. Too often they were getting into trouble with the law. By providing them with employment and a clean and healthy work environment, we could make a difference. If we could divert our young people from heading in the wrong direction, we could very well prevent more serious problems in the future.

In consultation with Governor Jerry Brown, he suggested that Senator Jerry Smith from Santa Clara, be the principal author with me as the principal co-author. I knew Senator Smith to be well respected and had no objections. Together, we worked the bill as it moved slowly through both Houses. Some members opposed. They were concerned we were developing a "socialistic program." This was not the case. This was a work program for young adults with the potential to yield our state a tremendous return on a relatively small investment.

Nevertheless, we were forced to make some amendments. In order to gain the necessary votes for approval, we introduced the California Conservation Corps as a pilot program. It was given a sunset clause, allowing the program to exist only until January 1, 1981. It passed with a two-thirds majority and Governor Brown signed the bill on July 7, 1976.

"Up From Second Street"   Ruben S. Ayala

The California Conservation Corps became official with an initial appropriation of $5,000,000.

The Corps' first years were not auspicious ones. The CCC encountered difficulty getting organized and setting up living quarters in camps throughout the State. However, despite the management difficulties, there was no problem recruiting young men and women for the program. In fact, more young people applied than could be accommodated. In 1979, Governor Brown appointed Brien T. Collins, his well respected legislative lobbyist, to step in and direct the Corps. It was his challenge to make the Corps successful.

B.T. Collins was colorful, outspoken and, more importantly, an effective organizer and motivator of young people. He had been a Green Beret during the Vietnam War. He had lost a hand, a leg and his sight in one eye. In spite of his obvious physical challenges, or maybe because of them, after his honorable discharge from the Army, B. T. finished his high school education and went on to graduate from the Santa Clara University School of Law.

As the Corps' Director, B.T Collins was clear in his message to the recruits. To the applicants he wrote the following: "Dear CCC Applicant, the CCC is a WORK program. You will do dirty backbreaking work and no one will thank you for it. The CCC is not a summer camp ... the most important skill you will learn is how to work hard ... You will work in rain, high winds, intense heat, snow, mud and cold mountain streams ... Above all, you must accept supervision. You must follow instructions." It was B.T. Collins who coined one of the Corps' mottos, "Hard work, low pay, miserable conditions!"

Despite his sometimes-blunt approach, he inspired the recruits as no other had. B.T.'s comments were often an inspirational highlight for the members of the Corp. One alumnus remembered B.T. as saying, "It's not the fanciest car or the foxiest chick that matters. Is the world any better because you were there?"

B.T. Collins served as Director of the California Conservation Corps through 1981. During his tenure, a cost/benefit study was commissioned. It demonstrated that for every $1 spent on the CCC, the State of California benefited $1.65. By 1983, a follow-up cost/benefit study revealed that the return on every dollar spent had increased to $1.77. Clearly the CCC was demonstrating its value and long-term viability.

B.T. Collins will always be remembered for his 1981 address to nearly 1,000 corpsmembers at the Santa Clara County Fairgrounds. At the time, there was a lot of public concern about the spraying of malathion on fruit trees to battle the Mediterranean Fruit Fly problem. Corpsmembers worked outdoors and were often exposed to the chemical in the sprayed areas. They had concerns about the potential negative effects of exposure to their own health. In a bold move, B.T. Collins raised a cup of malathion mixture up high in front of the large gathering and drank it. He was confident that the Corpsmembers were not being exposed to any significant danger. He had no apparent negative health effects from drinking the malthion. It was his way of relieving everyone's concerns. However, I don't recommend anyone try this.

In 1981, B.T. Collins accepted the position of Chief of Staff for Governor Brown. In an emotional goodbye, he thanked all present for the privilege of working with such hard working and dedicated individuals. In 1990, he was elected as a State Assemblyman from the Sacramento area. B.T. Collins passed away in 1993, still in office, at the age of 53. Since B.T.'s passing, CCC headquarters has been appropriately named the B.T. Collins California Conservation Corps Headquarters. Today, his statue stands in the foyer of CCC headquarters.

Since the original legislation creating the CCC held a sunset clause, I sponsored SB 1321 to reauthorize the California

Conservation Corps for another five years. By this time, Senator Smith had been appointed to the California Appellate Court in San Francisco. B.T. Collins and I worked together lobbying the bill to get the measure to the Governor for his signature. One skeptical legislator's support was won after a CCC crew saved a mobile home park in his district by sandbagging around it to protect it from rising floodwaters. With bipartisan support of a two-thirds majority, Governor Brown signed the reauthorization bill on March 27, 1980.

Under the outstanding, yet firm leadership of Collins, the CCC became a disciplined and well-respected agency. His legacy continues on. Today, the California Conservation Corps is the oldest and largest conservation corps in the world. Over 90,000 young people have served in the Corps since its inception, working to keep California beautiful. They have also assisted with emergencies, such as earthquakes, fires and floods. The best part about the Corps is the difference it has made and the values it has instilled in tens of thousands of our youth. California is clearly better off because of the California Conservation Corps. Besides making California a better place, the California Conservation Corps has set the standard for other states and even other nations. The California Conservation Corps became a permanent state department on September 29, 1983 with Governor Deukmejian's signature. Even during more partisan times, the CCC continues to enjoy support from both political parties. "The California Conservation Corps engages young men and women in meaningful work, public service and educational activities that assist them in becoming more responsible citizens, while protecting and enhancing California's environment, human resources and communities." (www.ccc.ca.gov)

At an anniversary event for the CCC, I was named "Father of the California Conservation Corps." I was delighted by the honor and still cherish the baseball cap they gave me with the embroidered title - "Ruben S. Ayala, Father of the C.C.C."

IN-LIEU TAX (VLF) STATE CONSTITUTIONAL AMENDMENT

As an elected local government official, it always frustrated me that local governments never knew how much of the in-lieu tax (fees imposed in place of taxes), collected by the State, would be returned to them to help balance their budgets. The in-lieu tax is the same as a motor vehicle license fee or VLF, which is the fee charged on the ownership of a registered vehicle in California. This fee is in-lieu of a personal property tax. Before 1940, local governments imposed a personal property tax on a household's personal property including motor vehicles. As of January 1, 1936 motor vehicles were no longer subject to the personal property tax administered by local governments. In the 1940's, all personal property taxes were a revenue source for local governments. Beginning in 1936, instead of each county imposing a varied property tax on motor vehicles, the state imposed the VLF to create a uniform system of taxation. California initiated a motor vehicle tax on all personal vehicle owners throughout the state at the same rate of 1.75% of the value of their vehicle on an annual basis. The revenues were returned to local governments based on population for their discretionary use. The Vehicle License Fee was increased to 2% in 1948.

While revenues from the VLF were historically returned to local governments, the state, when faced with difficult budgetary years, began to withhold portions of the revenues to fill its own coffers. From 1981 to 1983, state legislators returned only 66% of the VLF's revenues to cities, counties and special districts, diverting 34% to help balance the state's budget. In 1983, I introduced "a resolution to propose to the people of the State of California an amendment to the Constitution of the state, by adding Section 15 to Article XI thereof, relating to financing." (S.C.A. No. 23, 1983 Regular Session)

Sections 15 to Article XI reads as follows, "(a) All revenues from taxes imposed pursuant to the Vehicle License Fee Law, or its successor, other than fees on trailer coaches and mobilhomes, over and above the costs of collection and any refunds authorized by law, shall be allocated to counties and cities according to statute. (b) This section shall apply to those taxes imposed pursuant to that law on and after July 1 following the approval of this section by the voters."

Initially, I met with some opposition. I recall Assemblyman John Vasconcellos from Santa Clara asking me if I knew what I was doing. He thought that my proposed state constitutional amendment would balloon the state's budget deficit. He thought I was being fiscally irresponsible. I told him that having served so many years at the local level that I knew exactly what I was doing. I explained to him the challenges local governments were facing in balancing their own budgets, especially when they were never quite sure how much money the state was going to decide to pass on to them or when the funds would be made available. I reminded him that revenues generated from the vehicle license fee were historically local taxes and should remain so. I also expressed my opinion that the state had exercised far too much liberty in utilizing these funds for its own uses. S.C.A. 23 would protect and revitalize weakened local government services, such as law enforcement and fire protection. I said that these were some of the core services my constituents cared about most because these were the kind of services that most affected the quality of their lives. Yes, I told him, I understood exactly what I was doing.

In order to amend the state constitution, at least two-thirds of the members of the Assembly and the Senate had to first support S.C.A. 23 in order for it to appear on a statewide ballot to be voted on by the public. After some opposition, but with the strong support of the League of California Cities, the

proposed amendment was finally presented in 1986 directly to
the voters for final passage as Proposition 47. The proposition
was titled, "ALLOCATION OF VEHICLE LICENSE FEE
TAXES TO COUNTIES AND CITIES." It passed with overwhelming support. The final count was 3,487,604 votes in
favor to 775,437 votes against.

As of 2003, the California State Constitution continued
to require that all revenues generated from the Vehicle License
Fee (in-lieu tax), minus administrative costs, be distributed to
local governments. Due to my efforts in this cause, the League
of California Cities honored me in 1986 with the "Legislator of
the Year Award." I was very pleased with the results of our
efforts.

Some would argue that Governor Gray Davis lost his
bid to stay in office against the 2003 recall, because, in part, he
allowed the VLF to triple overnight. It's important to understand the history of the VLF to appreciate why he may have
made such a decision. More than ten years after the passing of
Proposition 47, the California State budget was enjoying a
budget surplus. Governor Wilson, before ending his second
term, wanted to cut taxes. He focused on the Vehicle License
Fee, even though, in theory, it wasn't the state's money to cut.
To gain support from local governments, he promised them
legislation that would continue to provide them the same
amount of money, based on the established formula. The
amount cut from the VLF would be "backfilled" with the state
budget surplus. Cities and counties were also assured by law,
that if in future years the state budget ran out of surplus
money, that a "trigger" would restore the VLF to its previous
"uncut" levels so that local government would not face a drastic
reduction in revenues.

Governor Wilson gained the necessary support and the
VLF was cut by a third. For some years, Californians personally benefited from the cut to the VLF. But, as the state budget

fell into an unprecedented deficit, the $4 billion or so from the state budget required each year to "backfill" revenues to cities and counties was difficult to come by. In response, Governor Davis allowed the VLF to triple in the summer of 2003, restoring the VLF to previous levels and relieving the state budget from the "backfill" requirement. This was quite a shock to vehicle owners in California. Newly elected Governor Arnold Schwarzenegger quickly reversed the action. I do believe we will be hearing more of this issue in the future.

DRIVE-BY SHOOTING BILL

During the early 1990s, a rash of senseless and mindless "Drive-By" shootings became far too frequent. This activity was mostly associated with teenagers, especially gang members. In 1993, I introduced Senate Bill No. 310. Approved by Governor Wilson on September 29, 1993, it was a first step to amend Section 190.2 of the Penal Code. Because this bill would amend a previously passed initiative measure, amending it would require the majority support of voters.

Before I began this process, there were nineteen elements or special circumstances that, when found to be true under a murder conviction, would call for the death penalty or life imprisonment without parole. Murder by means of a "Drive-By" shooting was not one of them. My bill added what is today the 21st element or special circumstance. It reads as follows, "The penalty for a defendant who is found guilty of murder in the first degree shall be death or imprisonment in the state prison for life without the possibility of parole if one or more of the following special circumstances has been found under Section 190.4 to be true: (21) The murder was intentional and perpetrated by means of discharging a firearm from a motor vehicle, intentionally at another person or persons outside the vehicle with the intent to inflict death."

In a follow-up piece of legislation I authored in 1995,

SB 9 (Ayala) was joined with SB 32 (Peace) to add what are today the 20th and 22nd elements or special circumstances that qualify a person convicted of murder in the first degree to death or life in prison without parole. Carjacking was also added to the 17th element's list of accompanying felonies to qualify for the death penalty or life in prison without parole. The added 20th special circumstance is if: "The victim was a juror in any court of record in the local, state, or federal system in this or any other state, and the murder was intentionally carried out in retaliation for, or to prevent the performance of, the victim's official duties." The added 22nd special circumstance is if: "The defendant intentionally killed the victim while the defendant was an active participant in a criminal street gang, as defined in subdivision (f) of Section 186.22, and the murder was carried out to further the activities of the criminal street gang."

Both bills passed both houses with a significant majority vote. Governor Wilson approved SB32 and SB9 in 1995, on September 26th and 27th, respectively. Again, for either bill to become law, each would have to be ratified by the popular vote. Proposition 196 and 195, representing the intent of SB 310, SB 9 and SB 32 went before the voters in 1996. Both Propositions passed.

Until 1996, the law allowed for a maximum 25 year to life sentence for a person convicted of first-degree murder during a "Drive-By" shooting or Carjacking. Under previous law, the sentence could be reduced by one-half with work-time credits and good behavior. To me, the maximum allowable sentence and its option for lenient probation didn't seem proportional to the severity of the crime. I thought it was important to send a clear message to perpetrators and would-be perpetrators that such behavior would not be tolerated. My hope was to discourage and help prevent such irrational behavior as Drive-By shootings, Carjacking and the like.

THE DRAM SHOP BILL

Early on in my Senate career, an individual was driving down from Mount Baldy and ran into a car traveling in the opposite direction. It was determined that the responsible party was driving under the influence of alcohol. Attorneys for the victims sued the intoxicated driver and the owner of the bar where the intoxicated driver had been previously served alcoholic beverages. The attorney representing the plaintiff, William Shernoff, won the landmark case and the owner of the bar was held financially liable.

As a result of this court decision, liability insurance rates for establishments serving alcoholic beverages skyrocketed. It forced some businesses to either cancel their liability coverage or not renew their policies. It forced some out of business.

At the request of restaurant owners, I introduced the Dram Shop Bill. It's important to clarify that at no time does this bill give the intoxicated driver any relief or reprieve from his or her individual responsibility. In fact, it strengthens the accountability of the intoxicated driver. My legislation declares, "that the furnishing of alcoholic beverages is not the proximate cause of injuries resulting from intoxication, but rather the consumption of alcoholic beverages is the proximate cause of injuries inflicted upon another by an intoxicated person. (c) No social host who furnishes alcoholic beverages to any person shall be held legally accountable for damages suffered by that person, or for injury to the person or property of, or death of, any third person, resulting from the consumption of those beverages." It also states, "(a) Every person who sells, furnishes ... any alcoholic beverage to any habitual or common drunkard or to any obviously intoxicated person is guilty of a misdemeanor." And it makes clear that "a cause of action may be brought by or on behalf of any person who has suffered injury or death against any person ... who sells, furnishes ... any alcoholic beverage … to any obviously intoxicated minor where the furnishing … of that beverage to the minor is the proximate cause of the personal injury or death sustained by that person."

Because it is not feasible for servers of alcoholic beverages to test their customers at the time of service to determine their blood alcohol level, it seemed reasonable to me that servers/owners of establishments who serve alcoholic beverages should not be held financially liable for the irresponsible behavior of the individual customers. The exception is when the customer is a minor, which is something that can be verified.

My proposed legislation made the trial lawyers go ballistic. They set forth a determined lobbying effort against the bill. I remember carrying the Dram Shop Bill through the Senate without too much difficulty. But then, when it arrived in committee on the Assembly side, support was almost evenly divided. I was counting on just one vote to get it through the committee and onto the Assembly floor for a final vote. In a last minute turn of events, the one vote I was counting on didn't show up, risking the passage of the bill through committee. As I considered my next option, Assemblyman Bill McVittie walked in. I had known Bill for many years. He was a trusted friend and colleague, but he was also an attorney. In fact, he had served as Chino's City Attorney for several years. His Assembly District was in my Senate District and we had worked together on many issues. I knew that as an attorney it would be difficult for Bill to support my bill, but he was my only chance. I approached him energetically. I told him that I knew he would be putting himself in a tight spot with the trial lawyers, but that I could really use his support. What a gentleman! He told me that he would vote for my bill in committee based upon the trust and the respect that he had for me, but that he would have to vote against it when it reached the floor. That was all I needed. Once approved by the committee, the bill went to the Assembly floor where I knew I had enough broad support to send the Dram Shop Bill to the Governor. In spite of continued intense lobbying by the legal profession, Governor Jerry Brown signed the bill in 1978 and it remains a part of California law today, more than twenty-five years later despite multiple and varied challenges by legislators.

Assemblyman Bill McVittie served three terms as Chino's Assemblyman (65th district) from 1974 to 1980. In March of 1979, Assemblyman McVittie was appointed by Governor Jerry Brown to the Los Angeles County Superior Court. He finished out his third term in the Assembly and took the bench immediately thereafter. In 2001, Judge McVittie retired from the bench. He told me recently that after voting "yes" on the Dram Shop bill in committee and "no" on the Assembly floor, that the trial lawyers wouldn't talk to him for months. Despite the sacrifice, he confirmed that this was a case where he valued our mutual trust over politics and that he would do it again if put to the test. I thanked him and assured him there would be no more such tests from me.

THE RALPH M. BROWN ACT - OPEN MEETINGS

On October 10, 1993, Governor Pete Wilson signed into law, Senate Bill 36, expanding the Ralph M. Brown Act requiring local government agencies to hold open meetings in California. The bill combined with SB 1140 and AB 1426 added nearly 5,000 words to the existing 6,000 words of legislation. I was one of SB 36's co-authors. Leading up to its passage, some local city officials opposed the idea of creating a more open environment for conducting their business. They claimed that under the proposed amendments they would not be able to handle personnel and legal issues behind closed doors. One Chino Hills City Councilman was quoted as saying that "whoever the idiot was that proposed the amendments had never served on a local board."

Senator Quentin Kopp from San Francisco, a personal friend, was the bill's principal author. I interviewed Senator Kopp on my first half-hour informational program, on Chino Valley Cablevision Channel 20. He responded to the local criticism by explaining that he had served on the San Francisco Board of Supervisors for more than fourteen years and that anybody making such criticism simply hadn't read the bill. As one of the bill's co-authors and a former member of the Chino Unified School Board, the Chino City Council and the San Bernardino County Board of Supervisors, I agreed with him.

California's original open meeting legislation, the Brown Act, was signed into law in 1953 by Governor Earl Warren. In 1961, the name of the legislation was changed to the "Ralph M. Brown Act." The opening paragraphs of the legislation well describes its intent, "In enacting this chapter, the Legislature finds and declares that the public commissions, boards and councils and the other public agencies in this State exist to aid in the conduct of the people's business. It is the intent of the law that their actions be taken openly and that their deliberations be conducted openly. The people of this State do not yield their sovereignty to the agencies which serve them. The people, in delegating authority, do not give their public servants the right to decide what is good for the people to know and what is not good for them to know. The people insist on remaining informed so that they may retain control over the instruments they have created."

While some may argue that open-meeting laws cost the public agencies money, or slow down the governing process, or create a lot of unnecessary hassle, I would simply say that history has taught us that transparency and public involvement in local government are essential to the well being of our communities. I believe the value of the Ralph M. Brown Act far exceeds its costs or inconveniences.

PROPOSITION 13

In 1978, California voters approved the "TAX LIMI-TATION - INITIATIVE CONSTITUTIONAL AMEND-MENT", otherwise known as Proposition 13. According to the Abbreviated Listing for Proposition 13, published by the California Secretary of State in 1978, "This initiative would: (1) place a limit on the amount of property taxes that could be collected by local governments [1% annually], (2) restrict the growth in the assessed value of property subject to taxation [2% annually with the assessed valuation base year set at 1975-76], (3) require a two-thirds vote of the Legislature to increase state tax revenues, and (4) authorize local governments to impose certain non-property taxes if two- thirds of the voters give their approval in a local election." In 1978, 64.8% of California voters approved Proposition 13 and it remains California law today.

Prior to the enactment of Proposition 13, property owners were at the mercy of County Tax Assessors, who at times, excessively increased assessed property values, thus raising tax liabilities to property owners. Some local governments also aggressively increased the property tax rates in their areas. Property owners on fixed incomes suffered the most. Anti-Tax champions, Paul Gann and Howard Jarvis, seized the opportunity, successfully gathering the required signatures to place Proposition 13 on the ballot. Since its passage over twenty-five years ago, Proposition 13 has withstood countless legal and political challenges. The success of Proposition 13 is also heralded for establishing the initiative process as an effective tool to bypass state government and go directly to the people to initiate change in state government. Its success also fueled a number of anti-tax movements nationwide.

As far as I know Proposition 39, passed in 2000, is the first successful measure to relax requirements of Proposition 13. Proposition 39, titled, "SCHOOL FACILITIES. 55% LOCAL VOTE. BONDS, TAXES. ACCOUNTABILITY REQUIREMENTS ..." lowered the voter approval standard to 55% to sell bonds "for the repair, construction, or replacement of school facilities..." It also added increased accountability standards such as requiring annual performance and financial audits on use of bond proceeds and the establishment of a Citizens' Bond Oversight Committee for each bond measure passed. On March 5, 2002, voters in the Chino Valley Unified School District approved the issuance of $150,000,000 of bonds for the modernization and renovation of existing school facilities and the construction of new school facilities. I've already seen improvements being made at existing school sites and new schools being built throughout the District. My son, Maurice, as one of the first members of the Citizens' Bond Oversight Committee, has kept me updated on ongoing projects. The Oversight Committee plays an essential role in looking out for taxpayers' interests.

Coming from local government and being a State Senator, I have to admit, I had my concerns about the potential negative effects of the passage of Proposition 13. A number of well-respected tax experts indicated to me that if Proposition 13 passed that education, city, county and special district (ie. fire districts) officials would be in Sacramento with their hats in their hands, pleading for state government assistance within three years. The tax experts were wrong. Local officials were crowding the State Capital's hallways within a year. Community Colleges were especially vulnerable, as a larger portion of their budget was dependent on local property taxes.

On the other hand, as a result of the passage of Proposition 13, senior Californians on fixed incomes are no longer faced with being taxed out of their homes. With a set formula, none of us has to worry about extreme increases in property taxes from year to year. For homeowners, Proposition 13 has been a godsend.

However, in the last twenty-five years, Proposition 13 has revealed some other unforeseen drawbacks. Under Proposition 13, each time a residential or commercial property is sold, its value is re-assessed to the most recent sales price, usually resulting in an increase in taxes for the new owners. Since homes are sold more frequently than commercial properties, their assessed values have also increased more often. As a result, residential property owners, as compared to commercial property owners, are paying a larger and larger portion of the total property tax bill.

Another drawback is that a new buyer purchasing a median priced house in California will have to pay nearly $500,000 for the same house that may have been valued at $50,000 for the base year 1975-1976. A neighbor, who paid $50,000 for the same floor plan and lot size in 1976 and has continued to live in the same house, is only required to pay around $800 a year for property taxes. A new buyer is required to pay at least $5,000 a year, or $4200 more. Yet, both households are provided the same city and county services. Despite the pros and cons, I believe Proposition 13 passed because too many local governments over-taxed their property owners.

As a homeowner myself, who is retired, I truly appreciate the benefits that Proposition 13 has afforded my wife, Irene and me. We've lived in our house since 1952 and enjoy an assessed property valuation based upon the base year of 1975-1976. However, after twenty-five years of experience with Proposition 13, I am convinced that if we sincerely revisit the issue, we will find areas of potential improvement and increased equity.

MILK PRODUCERS SECURITY TRUST FUND

In 1987, I authored a bill establishing the Milk Producers Security Trust Fund. In July of 1986, Knudsen Dairy failed to pay milk producers according to terms set out in long-term contracts. Knudsen Dairy was never able to make up the missed payments and eventually filed for bankruptcy protection. Chino Valley dairy farmers, along with other dairy farmers throughout the state of California, were negatively impacted from the resulting significant revenue loss. Some dairy farmers were forced into bankruptcy themselves.

The Milk Producers Security Trust Fund assesses charges on the milk handlers (ie. Knudsen), generating 110% of one month's milk purchases. The Director of the Food and Agriculture Department administers the trust fund. The fund pays dairymen for their milk in the event handlers default on their payments. As of 2003, the Milk Producers Trust Fund held around $19 million. For over 16 years, the trust fund has been an effective safety net for the dairy industry in California.

WESTERN UNIVERSITY

In 1980, I authored SB 1461, exempting Western University of Health Sciences in Pomona from the Code of Corporate Practices and Conduct. This allowed Western University to establish a non-profit medical clinic on campus, helping it become one of the largest full-fledged medical schools in California. Dr. Phillip Pumerantz founded Western University in 1977 and continues decades later as its President. According to Dr. Pumerantz, SB 1461 was instrumental in launching Western University Medical Center. With a vibrant medical center on campus, Western University is able to offer its students a practical education combined with a sound academic foundation.

Western University boasts over 4,500 successful alumni and growing. It has recently added a new program in veterinary medicine. Western University has been successful because of its primary commitment "to help students become compassionate and skillful caregivers."

BOYS REPUBLIC

Boys Republic, founded in 1907 by Mrs. Margaret Fowler and other prominent individuals, is a 200-acre institution in Chino Hills, CA. It's designed to assist at-risk young men learn to succeed through responsibility, accountability and accomplishment. In 1988, at the request of Chino Unified officials, I introduced SB 2874. This bill, signed by Governor Deukmejian on September 28, 1988, formally classified Boys Republic High School as "... a necessary small high school ... maintained by the Chino Unified School District in which ... the enrollment of the school is less than 200 pupils." (Education Code, Sec.42885.1.a).

More importantly, the bill provided and continues to provide, not only the actual daily attendance revenue for each student at Boys Reupublic, but an additional $180,000 a year to the Chino Unified School District for the quality educational services the District provides to students at Boys Republic. Prior to the legislation, the Chino Unified School District had been subsidizing the cost of providing educational services to Boys Republic. I believe this legislation has been a very positive contribution to the partnership of Boys Republic and Chino Unified as they work together to teach these students the skills necessary to live productive and meaningful lives. (Note: In 1997, Chino Unified became "Chino Valley Unified")

KEVIN COOPER AND SENSITIZED FENCE

In the 1980's, the California Institution for Men in Chino was having serious problems with escapees. In the summer of 1983, Franklin Douglas and Peggy Ann Ryen, their ten-year-old daughter, Jessica, their eight-year-old son, Joshua, and

Christopher Hughes, an eleven-year-old family friend staying
the night, were viciously attacked in their home in the middle of
the night. Joshua was the only survivor. Kevin Cooper, a
California Institution for Men escapee was soon the prime suspect.

Prior to this horrific tragedy, Governor Deukmejian had
been vigorously pressing the California State Legislature to
increase the community college fees. Senate Democrats were
unified in opposition to the Governor's proposed action.
During a late afternoon Democratic caucus (strategic meeting
of Senate Democratic members) called by then Senate Pro-Tem
David Roberti, Senator Roberti announced that after a long
exchange with the Governor, they had finally come to an agreement regarding the community college fee dispute. The
Governor had agreed to not raise fees for the community colleges in return for Senator Roberti's promise to allow for the
expansion of the prison population at the California Institution
for Men (C.I.M.) in Chino.

To me, the announcement was shocking. Interrupting,
I demanded to know why I had not been consulted since the
prison was located in my Senate District. I told them that a
good family had just been brutally murdered in the Chino Hills
area near the prison by a suspect believed to have been an
escapee from C.I.M. Moreover, C.I.M. was already overpopu-
lated. Understandably, my constituents were in shock and the
State's reply to my constituency was "more prisoners!" My
voice was getting louder and my tone even more serious. I
ended by loudly stating, "If that's all you care about the folks I
represent, then I'M IN THE WRONG PARTY!"

Senator Roberti then stated that he had given his word
to the Governor and that if the Democratic caucus didn't support his decision, then he was not their leader and would have
to resign his leadership position. I left the room and went
directly to my office and instructed my secretary, Edith Brewer,

to type my letter of resignation from the Democratic Party. I would become an Independent.

Early the next morning, Senator Roberti came to my office and informed me that he had decided to not give in to the Governor. He would support my position. As a result, I remained with the Democratic Party and Senator Roberti retained his leadership position and the population at C.I.M. was not expanded.

After the Senate session ended that year, I was speaking to a group of area businessmen at a luncheon at the Arbor Restaurant in Upland, Ca. Among the subjects covered at the luncheon was my exchange with Senator Roberti and the Democratic caucus. During the "question and answer" portion of the meeting, a member of the audience asked that since I had been so angry with the Democratic caucus, had I considered becoming a Republican? I quickly replied, "No, I was angry, but not that angry." The room erupted into laughter.

Kevin Cooper was convicted in 1985 of murdering Douglas, Peggy and Jessica Ryen and their house guest, Christopher Hughes. Kevin Cooper was sentenced to death. As of the publication of this book, Kevin Cooper was still sitting on Death Row. He was scheduled to be executed on February 9, 2004, but the Courts intervened just hours before his execution, opening up his conviction for further review.

After the tragedy in the Chino Hills area in 1983, I worked to improve the security conditions at C.I.M. It took me a couple of years after Kevin Cooper's escape to pass the funding legislation and to convince the Department of Corrections to install a sensitized fence at C.I.M. The fence was designed to set off an alarm, alerting correctional officials to escape attempts immediately. Also established was a warning system with Aerojet in the Chino Hills area. They agreed to place a warning beacon on top of a water tower on their hilltop property. In case of a prison escape, C.I.M. was to immediately inform Aerojet and they were to immediately light the warning beacon for all the surrounding communities to see. Some of us, however, felt that the beacon would not be of much help during foggy conditions or for those indoors. Nevertheless, these measures, combined with tighter security protocols inside C.I.M. dramatically cut down on successful escape attempts.

INTERSTATE/INTRASTATE TRAFFIC CODE AMENDMENT

At the request of "Spike" Hellman, then Commissioner of the Califorrnnia Highway Patrol, I introduced legislation amending the existing motor vehicle code to provide the same enforcement of drug and alcohol testing to interstate truck traffic as it did to intrastate truck traffic. Prior to this legislation, truck drivers on interstate highways were exempt from random drug and alcohol testing from CHP officers. Truck drivers on intrastate highways were not exempt. Commissioner Hellman felt the exemption was unjustified and represented a serious safety concern on the interstate highways throughout California. My legislation allowed for random drug and alcohol testing for truck drivers on both the interstate and intrastate highways throughout California. It also provided that taxi-cab drivers also be subject to random drug and alcohol testing. I believe that all of California's highways are safer as a result of this legislation.

FINGERPRINTING FOR CHILDREN

In April of 1994, I initiated a program of fingerprinting children. Our district staff, headed by our Project Manager, Martie Rodriguez, conducted the program in elementary schools throughout our Senate District. It was aimed at students from kindergarten through sixth grade whose parents had signed a permission slip in advance requesting that the fingerprinting take place. The parents were given their child's fingerprints for safekeeping. In the case of an emergency, where a child would be missing, the parents could then be prepared to present to the police a set of their child's fingerprints along with a cuurent photo of their child. These are often key in helping the police find missing children more quickly. Our staff and volunteers, such as Darlene Conley and the Marge Chacon family, visited 58 elementary schools in the Ontario, Montclair, Colton, Fontana and Chino School Districts. We also fingerprinted children at areas such as J. C. Penney and the parking lot of Sam's Club. On October 20, 1994 we reached a milestone. Tyler Moreno, a second grader at Howard Cattle Elementary School in Chino, became the 20,000th student to be fingerprinted through our efforts. We received many letters of appreciation from parents from all across the District.

CHINO VALLEY'S FIRST DIFIBRILLATOR

While trimming a tree in the backyard, I fell and broke my ankle. It was a compound fracture. Irene called 911 and Chino Valley Fire responded immediately. They were highly professional and I was very grateful for their prompt action. As soon as I was able, my staff and I organized a fundraiser. The proceeds were used to purchase Chino Valley Fire District's first defibrillator. It was my way of thanking Chino Valley Fire for the great service they continually provide our community.

ASSEMBLYMAN FRED AGUIAR and SUPERVISOR LARRY WALKER

Fred Aguiar and Larry Walker were two bright and intelligient young men aspiring to serve in elected public office when I first met them. Fred, a Vietnam Army veteran, was a successful Real Estate Broker working out of the Lee Alves Real Estate Office in Chino. Fred was also the President of the Chino Valley Chamber of Commerce. Under Fred's leadership

in 1976, the Chamber changed its name from the "Chino
Chamber of Commerce" to the "Chino Valley Chamber of
Commerce," reflecting a more expansive and inclusive
approach.

Both Fred and Larry graduated from Chino High
School. Larry was a recent graduate of the U.C.L.A. School of
Law, serving in the U.S. Naval Reserves and working as a
licensed Real Estate Broker. He was also working for
Assemblyman Bill McVittie as his field representative in Chino.

Both Fred and Larry approached me regarding my
endorsement for their campaigns for the upcoming 1978 Chino
City Council race. I faced a genuine dilemma. Leonard
Frketich and Angel Martinez were the two incumbents running
for re-election and both were personal friends of mine.
Leonard had even been involved supporting me in my campaign for Mayor. I felt torn. However, I also genuinely felt
that it was a good time to introduce some new ideas and new
personalities into city hall. Much to the distress of the incumbents, I publicly endorsed both Fred and Larry for the Chino
City Council seats and both were successful at getting elected.
Looking back, I clearly made the right decision.

Larry Walker went on to be elected Chino's Mayor in
1980 and served until 1986. In 1986, Larry was elected to the
San Bernardino County Board of Supervisors, serving as the
Chairman from 1991 to 1993. Larry served as a County
Supervisor until 1998 when he was elected as the San
Bernardino County's Auditor/Controller-Recorder. As of
2005, Larry Walker remained in that position.

Fred Aguiar replaced Larry as Mayor of Chino in 1986
and served until 1992. In 1992, Fred won a successful campaign for the 61st California State Assembly Seat.
Assemblyman Aguiar represented the 61st Assembly District
until 1998 when he reached his term limits. In 1998,
Assemblyman Aguiar became Supervisor Aguiar after being

elected to the San Bernardino County Board of Supervisors. From 2001 to 2003 Supervisor Aguiar served as Chairman of the Board of Supervisors for San Bernardino County.

On December 11, 2003, newly elected California Governor Schwarzenegger announced the appointment of Fred Aguiar as Secretary of the State and Consumer Services Agency. The Agency has an annual budget of more than $1.3 billion and employs around 15,000 people. SCSA, as it's known, is composed of many departments; The Department of Consumer Affairs, The Department of General Services, The Department of Fair Employment and Housing, The Franchise Tax Board, The California Public Employees' Retirement System, The California State Teachers' Retirement System, The California Science Center, The California African American Museum, The California Building Standards Commission, The State Personnel Board and The Office of Insurance Advisor. Concerning Fred's appointment, Governor Schwarzenegger said, "Fred's experience in government makes him a fantastic addition to my administration … I look forward to working with him to better serve the state." (www.schwarzenegger.com)

Personally, I think the Governor's choice was an excellent one. I'm glad to support Fred in his new position.

While Fred was in the Assembly and I was in the Senate, we worked together on a number of local issues. These included the successful completion of Highway 71 up to the Riverside County line and the naming of the improved highway, the "Chino Valley Freeway." We also worked on issues involving the California Institution for Men property and the expansion of Ayala Park. One of our more prominent legislative endeavors was the designation of Blue Ribbon Week in California. Working in conjunction with the City of Ontario, we jointly pushed through ACR 39, designating the week of

May 15 in California to recognize the sacrifices and efforts of all law enforcement officers in the State.

"UP FRONT WITH SENATOR RUBEN AYALA"

On Thursday, August 12, 1993, "Up Front With Senator Ruben Ayala" first aired on Channel 20 at 7 p.m. on Chino Valley Cablevision. It was a weekly interview program made available through cable services in Ontario, Rancho Cucamonga, Fontana and Rialto. For the next five years, until I retired in 1998, I hosted the weekly half-hour interview program. Its purpose was to bring state officials and legislators from Sacramento to give our District citizens the opportunity to hear their views and better understand the issues. I also felt it was important for our leaders in Sacramento to get to know our District personally and the issues most important to our constituents.

I remember my first interview was with Senator Quentin Kopp (I-San Francisco). Upon his visit, he noted how pleasantly surprised he was by the many corn fields throughout Chino and Chino Hills. He knew Chino was well known for its Dairy Industry, but didn't realize how much of the Chino Valley was dedicated to agriculture production at the time.

In our first interview, we discussed pending legislation that he had authored and I had co-authored concerning the expansion of the Ralph M. Brown Act, a law designed to ensure that governmental agencies conduct their business in front of the public. This makes the governing process more transparent and inviting to public involvement. He defended what he felt was uninformed criticism from a local city official towards the proposed improvements. Just two months later, the bill was signed into law by Governor Pete Wilson. At the end of our interview, I asked Senator Kopp to describe various political notables by responding with just one word. This format became a favorite and was dubbed the "Name Game." I began with "President Clinton." His answer was, "slick, articulate." Governor Wilson - "Dogged." Government - "Man with a sense of humor." Willie Brown - "Deft." Quentin Kopp - "Benevolent."

Over the next five years, I had the distinct pleasure of interviewing scores of political figures from Sacramento. I didn't care what party they represented. I just cared that the people in our District had a chance to hear from them and know how they stood on the issues most important to us. I interviewed Willie Brown, Gray Davis, Jim Brulte, Richard Mountjoy, Paul Horcher, Bill Jones, Dan Lungren, then CHP Commissioner Maurice Hannigan, and many more.

Playing the Name Game with Willie Brown, his answers were as follows: President Clinton - "Talented." Richard Mountjoy - "Young, Irresponsible." Pete Wilson - "Superb Technician." Jim Brulte - "Consensus Taker." Paul Horcher - "Independent." At the time, Willie Brown was in a tough fight for the Speakership of the Assembly. Richard Mountjoy, a Republican Assemblyman, was a staunch opponent, while Horcher, also a Republican Assemblyman, shocked the Republican party and his constituents when he cast a critical vote in support of Willie Brown and changed his party affiliation from Republican to "Decline to State."

About the same time, I interviewed both Mountjoy and Horcher. Mountjoy's replies to the Name Game revealed the ongoing tension and partisanship. Mountjoy answered as follows: President Clinton - "Weak." Newt Gingrich - "Strong." Bill Lockyer - "Pleasant." Willie Brown - "Schemer." Jim Brulte - "Consensus Taker." Paul Horcher - "Turncoat." Richard Mountjoy - "Pleasant."

Horcher's replies were equally revealing: President Clinton - "Embattled." Newt Gingrich - "Cocky." Pete Wilson - "Ambitious." Bill Lockyer - "Capable." Willie

Brown - "Mature." Jim Brulte - "Immature." Paul Horcher - "Independent." Richard Mountjoy - "Phony."

On one of the programs, I interviewed Jim Gomez, then the Director of California Department of Corrections. I took the opportunity to share with Mr. Gomez the success I had had in organizing a group of developers willing to purchase the 2,500 acres at the CIM facilities and the Hemen G. Stark Youth Training School in Chino. I emphasized that the money raised by the sale could then be used to build replacement state-of-the-art facilities in a less populated area.

Mr. Gomez flatly rejected my proposal, saying, "CIM is a very important prison to the state. We think CIM will probably be a prison for a long time." After the interview, I gave it another try. "I can't convince you?" I asked him off camera. He answered, "No, Chino is a good place." The closest I came to a real negotiation with Mr. Gomez was when he stated, "If you have a developer who wants to give me a check for $800 million, give me a call." Unfortunately, developers were only willing to pay the fair market value at the time, which was about $376 million or $150,000 an acre.

AYALA RESOLUTIONS
THE JANE FONDA RESOLUTION

During my tenure as a State Senator, I introduced three resolutions that received national attention. In 1979, I introduced THE JANE FONDA RESOLUTION. Governor Jerry Brown had appointed controversial movie personality Jane Fonda to the California Arts Council earlier in the year. The Senate Rules Committee had one year to confirm her appointment. They had been floundering for nearly four months, but were unable to make a decision. In the meantime, many legislators from both parties and from both houses of the legislature were receiving tremendous negative feedback from their constituents. By 1979, Jane Fonda's leftist stands and anti-war activities during the Vietnam conflict were well known. In 1972, many felt she had gone too far when she made her well-publicized friendly visit to North Vietnam during hostilities. She was photographed aiming skyward a Viet-Cong anti-aircraft gun used to fire at American aircraft. In 1988, in an interview with Barbara Walters on 20/20, Jane Fonda publicly apologized for her activities in North Vietnam, characterizing them as, "thoughtless and careless." Unfortunately, at the time of her appointment in 1979, she did not demonstrate nor had she demonstrated any regret for her anti-American activities.

On the last day of the Senate session that year, I stood on the Senate floor and made the motion for Jane Fonda to be removed from the California Arts Council. My motion caught many senators by complete surprise. There was momentary chaos. Senator Lou Cusanovich, who was presiding at the time, immediately took control of the meeting and restored order. He then calmly announced that he would allow three senators to speak in support of the Ayala motion and three members to speak in opposition. He would further allow me, as the maker of the motion, to offer the closing remarks.

The debate was mostly ideological. Senator Robert Nimmo from Atascadero, emphasized that Jane Fonda had gone to Hanoi in Vietnam and given aid and comfort to the enemy during a time of open hostilities between our nations. He indicated that, according to his upbringing, she qualified as a traitor to the United States of America.

In support of Jane Fonda, Senator Diane Watson from Los Angeles spelled out a long list of awards Ms. Fonda had received from the Performing Arts Community throughout her career. She felt that Jane Fonda was an excellent candidate to serve on the California Arts Council.

Senator Ray Johnson from Chico felt otherwise. To his fellow senators, he said, "Both Senator Ayala and I have sons who fought in Vietnam. Jane Fonda's visit to Hanoi during hostilities and her behavior there are, to me, unforgivable."

In my closing statement, I explained that a Governor's appointment quite often is two-fold. It is an honor given to a qualified person, and at times, it is an honor granted for political gain. I reminded the members of the Senate that California should not obligate itself to honor anyone who had given aid and comfort to our enemy during a time of open hostilities. The Jane Fondas of our country did not deserve to be honored by our government.

A roll call vote was taken and only 5 senators voted against the motion. Governor Brown was furious and was quoted as characterizing us as "lacking guts" and caring more for our own political futures than doing what he believed to be the right thing. In the days to follow, I received over 2,000 letters from all over the country. Except for about 18 or 20 letters, they were all in full support of my action to remove Jane Fonda from the California Arts Council. One correspondence I fondly remember was a postcard from a Mr. Nichols, a residence of Upland, California. The gentleman simply wrote, "Senator, you done good."

I received a more sober letter from Henry Fonda, Ms. Fonda's father. As would be expected, he wrote to defend and support his daughter. In my response to Mr. Fonda, I ended my letter by saying that while he supported his daughter, I supported my son and all the other Americans who fought and died in Vietnam.

Incidentally, during the Vietnam crisis, California State employees, who were members of the California State Military Reserves, were obligated to serve full time under the jurisdiction of the United States Army. Not only were they separated from their families for extended lengths of time, but they had to leave their State salaried jobs for a much smaller paying position in the U.S. Army. Many of them faced financial hardship as they remained obligated to pay their mortgages and support their families. Recognizing a legitimate need, I introduced legislation, which was later signed into law by Governor Brown, which paid the difference between their Army pay and their State salary pay, allowing them to serve their country with dignity and security.

THE SIRHAN SIRHAN RESOLUTION

My second resolution was directed to the California Parole Board. Sirhan Sirhan, who had been tried and convicted of assassinating Presidential Candidate and U.S. Senator Robert F. Kennedy in 1968, was requesting the Parole Board release him from prison. I introduced a resolution urging the Parole Board not to release him at anytime. Ted Koppel with KABC interviewed me on ABC News Nightline for the story. The Senate passed the resolution unanimously. As Chairman of the State Prison Management Committee, I later made a visit to the state prison in Corcoran, California. While there, I personally observed Sirhan Sirhan, Juan Corona and Charles Manson securely behind bars. All three were segregated from the general prison population.

THE BATAAN DEFENDERS RESOLUTION

My third resolution memorialized the tens of thousands of U.S. and Filipino troops who suffered beyond belief as they fought to defend the Bataan Peninsula on the Island of Luzon in the Philippines during WWII. Just days after the bombing of Pearl Harbor, the Japanese landed on the Island of Luzon with a formidable invading force. Unprepared to defend an all-out invasion, tens of thousands of U.S. and Filipino soldiers retreated to the Bataan Peninsula on the island. One of their greatest challenges was their lack of adequate supplies. This band of defenders held out in the isolated jungles for four months against tremendous Japanese forces until they finally ran out of food, ammunition and medical supplies. On April 9, 1942, Lieutenant General Jonathan Wainwright ordered his men to cease-fire and surrender. Thousands of fatigued, wounded and ailing American and Filipino war prisoners were forced to march through dense jungle more than 60 miles to the Japanese prison camp.

"Julio Barela recalled in his autobiography, 'In the eyes of the Japanese, we were cowards to have surrendered as they believed that taking your own life was a far better fate. We were beaten, slapped, pushed, tortured and yelled at while we marched. I was struck on the back of the head with the butt of the rifle of one of my captors. I remembered thinking of my mother and how she would suffer if I died. So I balanced as much as I could so as not to fall. Once an American soldier would fall, he would be stabbed with the bayonet or shot. Several of my comrades fell from fatigue on top of illness and would not go on. They were immediately killed.
All the time I thought I would be next.'" (http://reta.nmsu.edu:16080/bataan/curriculum/introduction/history.html)

Hundreds of ailing and wounded men died of thirst, starvation and lack of medical treatment en route. Upon arriving at the prison camp, 54,000 beleaguered soldiers were packed into the Japanese prison camp, Camp O'Donnell, designed to accommodate just 10,000. Hundreds more perished. Their cruel forced march became known as the Bataan Death March.

"The POWs were greeted by the Japanese commandant of Camp O'Donnell, who, as Weldon Hamilton recalled, gave the survivors a chilling and short speech. He said 'We are enemies. We shall always be enemies. The only thing I am concerned of is how many of you are dead every morning.' Hamilton remembered the commandant adding that the survivors should envy those who died on the Death March, 'for they are the lucky ones.'" (http://reta.nmsu.edu:16080/bataan/curriculum/introduction/history.html)

In all, only a third of the Bataan POW's survived. Most spent the rest of the war suffering from one Japanese prison camp to another. The inhumanity and cruelty of the Japanese towards its prisoners of war during WWII is nothing short of horrific.

We can never forget the agonies endured and heroism demonstrated by the Bataan Defenders. I introduced this resolution on the floor of the California State Senate in order to help ensure that the Bataan Defenders are never forgotten. The resolution passed without opposition.

"Up From Second Street"   Ruben S. Ayala

CHAPTER TEN

THOUGHTS AND REFLECTIONS

NOTABLE INTRODUCTIONS

I have fond memories of my time on the Senate floor. Two of my most memorable occurrences did not involve approval of any legislative effort. Rather, it was the honor of introducing two famous and special individuals who I hold in very high regard. One was retired Marine Corps Colonel Mitchell Paige. Colonel Paige was a Platoon Sergeant when he earned the Congressional Medal of Honor on October 26, 1942. Paige earned our nation's highest military award while serving with the First Marine Division on the enemy-held island of Guadalcanal in the Solomon Islands. He was in command of 33 Marines spread across a ridge with just a few machine guns left in their arsenal. Their job was to defend the ridge through the night until reinforcements could arrive. Facing an onslaught of thousands of Japanese soldiers in several night-time raids, he and his men continually fired at enemy forces until Sergeant Paige was the last able-bodied American fighter left. As morning approached, he ran from machine gun to machine gun, laying down fire across the ridge to fool the enemy into thinking they were facing a stronger defense. Finally, reinforcements arrived. Instead of falling back out of the battle for a well-deserved respite, Sergeant Paige charged forward with machine gun in hand until the enemy began its retreat.

153

In 1942, President Franklin D. Roosevelt presented Sergeant Paige with the Congressional Medal of Honor. It reads in part, "For his extraordinary heroism and conspicuous gallantry in action against the enemy above and beyond the call of duty while serving with the Second Battalion, Seventh Marines, First Marine Division. His great personal valor and unyielding devotion to duty were in keeping with the highest traditions of the United States Naval service." Colonel Paige was my Company Commander when I returned to the States at the Marine Rest Camp in Klamath Falls, Oregon. It was the highest honor to serve with him and years later to introduce him on the floor of the California State Senate. I was saddened to hear that Colonel Paige passed away on November 15, 2003 in his home in La Quinta, California. He was 85 years old.

The other notable person was the celebrated photographer, Joe Rosenthal. Mr. Rosenthal took the dramatic Pulitzer prize-winning photograph of the raising of the American flag on Mount Suribachi on Iwo Jima during World War II. That photo, which electrified the nation at the time and since, became the model for the huge monument now standing near the National Cemetery in Washington, D.C. One of Mr. Rosenthal's amusing and interesting stories was his disclosure that soon after the Japanese attack on Pearl Harbor, he attempted to join the Army, then the Navy and finally, the Air Corps. They all rejected him because he failed the physical examination. So he went to work for the Associated Press and ended up with the Marines in the jungles of the South Pacific. Mr. Rosenthal autographed my poster of the famous flag raising. I will always cherish it.

TEAMWORK

We've all heard the adage, "There's no 'I' in the word TEAM." And so it is with those who hold elected office. An elected full-time official is no more effective than the people on his support team. I was extremely fortunate to have people second to none, both in my District and Sacramento offices. Members of our team were loyal, honest, knowledgeable, compassionate, energetic and dedicated.

Mike Valles, who managed a number of our Senate races, was our first Chief of Staff in our District Office. Mike had previously worked for Assemblyman John Quimby's office and understood our District and State issues. He was also savvy and shrewd in political matters, an excellent organizer and was an overall invaluable resource in our organization.

After Mike, former San Bernardino City Police Chief Lou Fortuna served as our District Chief of Staff. When Lou retired, I promoted Wilma (Willie) Silva to the position. Willie had been my Secretary when I was Chairman of the San Bernardino County Board of Supervisors. As our Chief of Staff, Willie had the opportunity to reach her full potential and she met our expectations fully. She served exceptionally well as a good-will ambassador in the San Bernardino area of our District. Willie, her late brother and our Campaign Treasurer, Ed Young; Martin Matich, our unofficial Campaign Finance Manager; his late brother, Jack Matich; and George Borba from Chino, were all so well-known and respected and such staunch supporters that all of our campaign fund-raising events held at the Orange Show grounds were huge successes. At one point, Martin Matich, a well-respected Republican, was serving as our unofficial Campaign Finance Manager. At the same time, he was serving as the official Campaign Finance Manager for Governor Pete Wilson in the Inland Empire. Since I was a Democrat, Governor Wilson's organization approached Martin. They suggested that to some in the California Republican Party it appeared to be a conflict of interest for him to be working so closely with a Democratic Senator while working as the Campaign Finance Manager for Governor Pete Wilson. Interestingly enough, Martin agreed and resigned his position with Governor Pete Wilson's campaign. I was delighted to have his friendship and support.

After many successful years, Willie retired as our Chief of Staff. She went on to work part-time in the late Congressman George Brown's office, as well as in State Senator Nell Soto's Office. Retired California Highway Patrol Captain, Al Irwin, took Willie's place after she retired. Al was a thorough organizer and a keen disciplinarian. Much of his modus operandi was a carryover from his many years with the California Highway Patrol. One of his assigned projects was to find a suitable central location to combine the San Bernardino and Ontario District offices. Merging the two offices and having all of our District personnel under one roof allowed us to know what the left and right hands were doing. It made for a better organization with improved efficiency in serving our constituents. Al located a central office in Rancho Cucamonga and carried out the consolidation.

Al's previous experience as a California Highway Patrol Captain, being in charge of a large number of personnel, was definitely an asset to our organization. After some time and at his request, Al resigned as our Chief of Staff and returned to the position of Field Representative. I asked George Burden to accept the job in Al's place.

George had been Chief of Staff for Senator Cecil Green in Orange County. He turned out to be a stronger pro-labor advocate than I felt comfortable with and some office matters were just not going to my satisfaction. After a short time, George stepped down.

At that time, I promoted Sondra Elrod, then our District Office Secretary, to Chief of Staff. Sondra had had some political exposure as a volunteer of then Chino Mayor Fred Aguiar. Sondra was always poised and professional. She made a positive impression with the public. Being a native of the West End of our District, she knew the area well and maintained a very good rapport with local citizens. Under her leadership, our staff was always well prepared for our Friday morning office briefings. After my retirement, Sondra went on to become the Public Information Officer for the Inland Empire Utilities Agency.

Members of our District Staff who greatly contributed to our success and who went on to serve with Senator Soto are Marti Rodriguez, who would undoubtedly make an excellent Chief of Staff for any elected official; Frank Stallworth and Evelina Contreras, one of our original staff members. Members of equal quality were Frank Elder, my high school baseball coach and namesake for the Chino High School basketball gym; Paul Palsa, David Madsen, Don Crawford, Don Kipp, Bill Hill, Patti Aguiar, Bill Morales and Bob Ulloa.

In our Sacramento Office, I was fortunate to have an equally outstanding, efficient, loyal and dedicated team. Originally, I retained my predecessor Senator Coombs' personnel. Edith Brewer remained as Chief of Staff and Rooks Poteet remained as Bill Clerk and all around office worker. While both Edith and Rooks were excellent in performing their office duties, neither one displayed much propensity for politics. In this area, Mike Valles was always willing to help out. When Edith retired, Mike filled the Chief of Staff position temporarily until I assigned our Capitol Secretary, Sandra Miller, to those duties.

Sandy had had experience working in several legislators' offices, including Senator Barry Keene's and Senator Leroy Green's. Both Senators were politically well established. As a result, Sandy was well acquainted with the politics of the State Capitol. She knew most of the other Senators' staff members and the leading lobbyists in the Capitol, which was very helpful to me.

Years later, as a member of the Senate Rules Committee, I was assigned a large office on the fifth floor with a great view of the beautiful Capitol Park. I asked Sandy to assist me in planning the renovation of our office in order to house both our Senate office staff and our Agriculture and Water Committee staff. Sandy was well organized and insisted that the rest of the staff follow her example. Under Sandy's direction, the renovation went smoothly and I never went to the Senate Floor without having the necessary files in order. Over the years, lobbyists, who dealt with all of the Legislators' offices, often commented that we had the most competent office in the Capitol building. After I retired, Sandy Miller became the Buildings Operations Officer under Senate President Pro-Tempore John Burton.

Rose Baldo, who worked the office computer to prepare the daily file for my chores on the Senate floor, was also a tremendous asset. Rose later became a Deputy Sheriff in Sacramento County. As I mentioned at the outset, an elected full-time official is highly dependent on a quality team. To my credit and theirs, I believe I had the best.

A TALK WITH THE GOVERNOR

A welcomed scenario developed during Governor Pete Wilson's last bill signing session in 1998. One of his staff members called my office to inquire if I would patricipate in a photo-op with the Governor. He would be signing my last piece of legislation. We were both about to retire. I remember thinking, "What a class act on the part of the Governor!" I flew to Sacramento for the occasion. When I walked into his office, he was sitting behind a large table with stacks of bills surrounding him. When I neared his table he looked up and smiled. I think it was the first time that he smiled at me. Throughout the photo session, he was amiable and we carried on a good natured conversation.

After the photo session, the Governor excused his staff and the photographers, saying that he wanted to have a few minutes alone. When everyone else had left the office, the Governor proceeded to tell me that he really liked and respected me. For one thing, he said, we had a bond since we were both former Marines. But then he told me how disappointed he was because, as a member of the Senate Rules Committee, I had not voted to approve some of his appointments.

The Governor let me know in no uncertain terms that the California State Constitution provides for the Governor to make appointments until the very last minute of his term. I didn't disagree with him, even though he had already signed my bill. However, I politely explained that the same source that grants the appointment authority to the Governor also designates the Senate Rules Committee to act as a check and balance to the Governor's appointments. The Senate Rules Committee has the responsibility to confirm or deny the Governor's nominees. I, in turn, told him that I believed that the Committee should not be a rubber stamp for any Governor. I reminded Governor Wilson that I had supported many of his selections, even when I felt the wrath of my fellow Democrats. He then asked me about my future plans and I asked him if he thought he might run for the U.S. Presidency again. He told me he had no such plans. We shook hands and wished each other well.

DEMOCRACY IN ACTION

Sir Winston Churchill, former Prime Minister of Great Britain and a most forceful leader during World War II, is quoted as stating, "...No one pretends that democracy is perfect or all-wise. Indeed, it has been said that democracy is the worst form of government except all the others that have been tried from time to time." (Hansard, November 11, 1947)

I have absolutely no quarrel with that statement. In our state and federal government, neither of the two major political parties is right in their position, on every issue, all the time. Inflexible and uncompromising members of both major political parties are not reason-based. Yet, there are too many such members, too often, dominating the public debate. These folks believe in, what I call the "cookie cutter" form of governance, meaning they believe that everyone else's philosophy should be made to conform to their own. They are often unyielding and uncompromising. As a result, they often are the cause of unnecessary gridlock and lack of responsiveness on the part of government to the needs of its people.

In our majority two-party system, winning candidates to the legislative bodies at the state and federal levels, often feel an obligation to follow the direction of party leaders when it comes to casting key votes. After all, most candidates depend on their party and party leaders for financial and logistical support during an election. The winning legislative candidates who are members of the majority party are further given special consideration for office space and staffing needs. If a legislator stands out on key issues, or has developed seniority, then there is a good possibility that he or she may also be appointed to a "juice committee." A juice committee is a prominent committee that attracts larger contributions from special interests to a legislator's campaign fund. The system has been designed to induce loyalty among party members.

However, there will be times when the party leaders believe they have sufficient votes to carry a measure. A legislator is sometimes allowed to vote independently (against the party line) if it's believed that there will be a backlash in his or her district in the next election. The paradox is that when a veteran legislator reaches a secure position in his or her own district, meaning they can get re-elected with or without party support, they then have seniority and are part of the leadership. Who wants to give that up? Most don't, so they remain dominated by party dogma. In the case of term limits, a legislator doesn't have the time to become independent, therefore, most legislators are beholden to their party's leadership and/or special interests during their time of service.

I may sound as if I'm complaining, but I am not. I am, however, explaining some realities of state and federal politics today. Despite the obvious problems in our majority two party system, I honestly believe that the United States of America has developed the most successful constitutional and representative form of governance in the history of the world.

That does not mean that all is well and that we, as private citizens, should abdicate our responsibility to be involved in the governing process. Our most fundamental responsibility as good citizens is to make sure we are informed and vote. I, like many, am greatly disappointed by continually low voter turnout at our elections. Some may think that their vote doesn't count. Let me tell you the power of just one vote. Adolf Hitler became the leader of the Nazi Party in 1923 by just one vote. Consider that just two more votes to the contrary may have prevented the mass murder of millions of innocent human beings. By less than one vote per precinct, John F. Kennedy was elected as President of the United States in 1960. More recently, in the Presidential Election of 2000, George W. Bush was very grateful for a relatively few number of votes in Florida that won him just enough electoral votes to win the Presidency, despite not winning the nation's popular vote.

I will always be grateful for the support I've been given by the Democrats and the large number of Republican votes I've received during my many successful election campaigns. In retrospect, I believe, I was somewhat of an enigma to members of both major political parties in Sacramento. I was too conservative for some Democratic colleagues and too liberal for some Republican friends. My primary committment was to always represent the majority of my constituents, regardless of their party affiliation. I remain fully convinced that serving our fellowman in Public Service is a noble profession. After 43 years as an elected official, I have no regrets about contributing the larger part of my life to Public Service.

On my last day on the Senate floor, as is the custom when a Senator retires, Senate Pro-Tem Leader John Burton presented me with a beautiful resolution, acknowledging my contributions. This was especially meaningful because we had had our differences. Members from both sides of the aisle surprisingly stood and expressed some very nice thoughts about me, including State Senator Tom Hayden, a liberal Democrat and a former husband to Jane Fonda. We had disagreed on a number of key issues. Despite our disagreements, Tom said concerning me, "He was the kind of person you read about in the American storybooks." Tom also announced he had become a converted Ayala fan. My response to the flattery was, "Now they tell me how good I was."

A couple of weeks before my term was over, Senator Burton stopped me in the hallway. He informed me that upon my retirement, I would have first choice of serving on a commission or board that had an opening. I was pleasantly surprised that the Senator would offer me the opportunity. We had bucked heads a number of times on the Senate Rules Committee.

I decided that since western San Bernardino County was one of the fastest growing areas in the State, with a tremendous dairy industry, an enormous challenge existed in acquiring acceptable land to dispose of the increasing sludge matter and dairy waste. The more the State delayed solving this serious problem, the higher the cost to the taxpayer would be.

I notified Pro-Tem Burton that my first Board choice

would be to serve on the California Waste Management Board. I felt that I would be effective working through the bureaucracy to solve one of San Bernardino County's more serious waste management problems. Senator Burton's response was, "You got it."

A few days after the session was over, I was admitted to the Chino Valley Medical Center emergency room for a medical problem requiring surgery. While there, I received a call from Senator Burton inquiring about my health. I thought, "How nice of John to call." But there was more to his call than a kind inquiry. Senator Burton went on to inform me he had bad news. He said he had been getting opposition to my appointment to the Waste Management Board from the environmentalists because, for one, I had authored the legislation authorizing the construction of the Peripheral Canal. The environmentalists had been very much opposed to the water project and obviously, they were still opposed to me. Before I could express my views on the matter, Senator Burton explained that Senator David Roberti's term on the California Unemployment Insurance Appeals Board (CUIAB) was ending and he would appoint Senator Roberti to the Waste Management Board and gladly appoint me to his previous post.

I served on the CUIAB from December 1998 until December 2002. This particular Board was a complete change of pace from anything I had ever experienced. Without any fanfare, this relatively obscure Board administers a vital program to a large number of our citizens. It provides financial benefits to individuals who are unemployed through no fault of their own. It consists of seven members, five appointed by the Governor, of which at least three must be attorneys. The State Senate and Assembly each appoint one member.

The Board's function is to hear appeals from either the employers or employees involved in claims for unemployment benefits. Although state and federal governments absorb the administrative costs of the program, employers pay for all benefits to employees through the employers tax assessment. The laws governing the unemployment insurance program, for the most part, are fair to both employer and employee. However, there are many instances when they favor the employee.

I must say I truly enjoyed my four years with the CUIAB. I found my fellow board members, judges, administrators and staff personnel to be wholly dedicated to the task. I hold them all in high regard, especially my secretaries, Irma Lowe in my Sacramento office and Gail Creech in my District office, who were both extremely helpful in getting me started in my new endeavor.

CHAPTER ELEVEN

MI FAMILIA Y HONORES

Our oldest son, Bud, attended Chino High School, where he played football and baseball and graduated in 1965. While a student at Mt. San Antonio College in Walnut, he was ordered to report to military duty. Bud did his basic training at Fort Ord, in Marina, California. He served as a Helicopter Door Gunner with the 25th Infantry Division of the U.S. Army, stationed in Cu Chi, Vietnam. For his exemplary service, Bud was awarded the Bronze Star Medal, the Combat Aircrew Wings and the Army Commendation Medal. After his honorable discharge, Bud enrolled at the University of La Verne in southern California, where he earned his Bachelor's Degree in Physical Education in 1972. He went on to graduate work at the University of La Verne and Chapman University. Bud has been a teacher and coach in the Chino Valley Unified School District for the past 30 years. In 1982, as the Tennis Coach for the Chino High School Tennis Team, Bud coached his team to win the school's only tennis league championship in its 100+ year history. He also coached for ten years as the Varsity Men's Head Tennis Coach at Mt. San Antonio College. Bud, whose first name is Ruben, spoke at the dedication of Ayala High School. He began his comments by expressing his gratitude for the honor bestowed upon his father and family. He then suggested that if the new school had been a 7th and 8th grade school, it could have been named the Ruben Ayala Jr. High

School. Bud and his wife, Jeanne, also a Chino Valley Unified teacher, live in Chino. Recently, I was delighted to find out that Jeanne had been transferred to teach Computer Science at Ayala High School.

Our son, Maurice, graduated from Chino High School in 1967. He ran for Student Body President his senior year and after a run-off election, he won. He was a member of the football, wrestling and track teams, setting school and league records in shot-putting. Maurice developed exceptional ability in Judo, studying at the Tenri Dojo. He was invited to the Olympic trials to compete in Olympic Judo for the 1980 Olympics. Unfortunately, the United States boycotted the Moscow Olympics and Maurice wasn't allowed to compete.

Maurice is also well known for his political activism. From 1974 to 1978, Maurice worked as Chief of Staff for William McVittie, Member, California State Legislature, 65th Assembly District. In 2000, Maurice was appointed as the District Director for California State Legislature, 61st Assembly District. He is currently working as a lobbyist in Sacramento and serves on the Citizens' Bond Oversight Committee for Measure M funds for the Chino Valley Unified School District. Maurice is a licensed commercial fisherman and a licensed stock and bond broker. He has a daughter, Danielle, who lives in Sacramento, California. Maurice and Tammie live in Chino Hills, California.

Our youngest son, Gary, also an alumnus of Chino High School, graduated in 1970. He competed on the wrestling team. After high school, he attended Chaffey College in Rancho Cucamonga and in 1975 earned his Bachelor's Degree in Communications and Marine Biology from California State University at Fullerton. He completed graduate work at the University of Southern California. Gary is a consultant on environmental and governmental construction for the National Hispanic Building Association (NHBA). For a time, Gary worked as a contributing photographer for the LA Times. His two daughters are Sarah Rose and Amy Elizabeth.

My oldest sister, Susie Delgado, lives in Chino with her husband, Vicente, and family. My younger sister, Estella Encinas, passed away two years go. Her husband, Maurice, lives in Alta Loma with one of their three daughters. "Maury" was the star baseball pitcher on our Pomona Junior College baseball team. Rosie Lara, my youngest sister, lives in Chino with her husband, Albert, and their family. My brother, Maury, lives with his wife, Kay, and their three sons in Eureka, California. My brother and sisters have always been there for me. I admire them greatly.

In July of 2005, Irene and I will celebrate our 60th wedding anniversay. In 1942, Irene graduated from Chino High School where she excelled in academics and athletics. Irene graduated from Chaffey College, where she was Student Body Secretary. She went on to graduate in 1947 from the California Hospital School of Nursing, then affiliated with the University of Southern California (USC). While at C.H.S.N. she was elected President of her senior class and served as a member of the United States Cadet Nurse Corps. Upon graduation, she worked as a nurse at the California Hospital in Los Angeles, CA. Two of our sons, Bud and Eddie, were born at the same hospital. Gary was later born at Pomona Valley Hospital. As a full time mother, Irene, cared for our growing family with love and dedication, while making time on a regular basis for her favorite hobbies, gardening and reading. As a member of the Confraternity of Christian Doctrine, Irene also made time to attend classes and teach elementary-age children. She also worked as a local Head Start teacher and taught in Adult School for several years. Irene later served on the Chino Valley Medical Center Citizens Advisory Board. For one year, she served as the Chairperson of the Board. While our children were in school, she was always active in the Parent Teacher

Associations and was the recipient of the Gird PTA Honory Life Award. She was also a favorite Den Mother to the Cub Scouts. Her tireless efforts, understanding and unquestionable support during our long and sometimes grueling campaigns (24 elections in all) were always in evidence and always made the difference. She is one of those indescribable and invaluable intangibles that too often are taken for granted in our busy lives. I cannot begin to imagine how limited our accomplishments would have been had we not been brought together. I remain forever grateful to my wonderful companion and partner in life, my wife, Irene.

No one knows what kind of life our family might have had if our grandparents had not come to the United States and settled in the Chino Valley of California in 1900. Not knowing the language, unsure of the circumstances, and yet, no obstacle was insurmountable. They hoped they were moving to a better life, where greater opportunity was within their reach for them and their children and grandchildren.

My grandparents, as did other immigrants, encountered a distinctly different cultural environment and language when they first arrived in Chino. The establishment in Chino, at the time, saw to it that Mexican newcomers only lived in a segregated setting. Yes, they experienced discrimination and economically, they were continually challenged. However, their aspirations were much less for themselves and much more for their posterity, and so they endured. Because of their convictions, love and support, their grandson was able to become a member of the Governing Board of their school district, their City Councilman, the Mayor of their city, the Supervisor of their County District, and finally, the State Senator of their California Senate District. While they were pleased that it happened, I don't think they were surprised. They already held the belief that in America, such things were possible.

While they may not have been surprised, I was and still

am. I never would have thought in my wildest imagination as a child of Mexican heritage growing up on Second Street in the Chino Barrio that I would meet and associate with some of our world's leaders. As a California State Senator, I was invited on multiple occasions to the White House to discuss urgent water-related issues and other concerns of Californians with Presidents Richard M. Nixon, Gerald R. Ford, Jimmy Carter and Ronald W. Reagan. In 1993, at a rally held at John Galvin Park in Ontario, California, I was asked to introduce Presidential Candidate, William J. Clinton. My wife and I were presented to Queen Elizabeth of England when she and her husband, Prince Phillip, visited the California State Senate. Irene thought the Prince was quite friendly and charming. On another occasion, I met with the soon-to-be Taiwanese President, Lee Teng-hui (a Cornell University Alumnus) to discuss the similarities of water problems facing Taiwan and California. After our lengthy discussion, he presented me with three autographed volumes he wrote concerning Taiwanese water issues. I donated the books to the Water Resources Institute at the California State University at San Bernardino.

A small group of Senators and our wives, while on our way to the Union of Soviet Socialist Republics, were the guests of the Finnish Parliament in Helsinki. I was very impressed with how sparkling clean and green Helsinki was. Water was everywhere. Living in a healthy environment was and still is a high priority to the Finnish people. I met, for the first time, a member of the Green Party. Party members shared concerns about being so close to the U.S.S.R. We were given special seating to watch the unicameral, 200-member Parliament, while they deliberated. Members are elected by a popular vote every four years. The 1952 Olympic games were held in Helsinki. Finland was the first country in Europe to allow women to vote. The food was great, especially the salads. To this day, Irene says the salads were edible works of art.

"Up From Second Street" Ruben S. Ayala

From Helsinki, we took the train to the Soviet Union. The train was dingy. At one stop, young Russian soldiers boarded our train and rudely inspected our train compartment. John Garamendi, then a State Senator, and his wife Patty shared our train compartment. We were disturbed by the unwarranted and disrespectful way we were treated.

We visited St. Petersburg and Kiev in the Ukraine, finally arriving in Moscow. Moscow was cold and it seemed it would snow at any minute. When we registered at the hotel, our passports were impounded and kept until it was time for our departure. This was before the Berlin Wall was torn down and Perestroika was initiated. We noted the results of government ownership and dominance of industry, banks, schools, agriculture, newspapers, radio, television, transportation, etc. Even the temperature in our rooms was controlled centrally from the hotel lobby. During our guided tours, we didn't see too many cheerful people in the streets of Moscow. The children looked healthy and cared for. The adults were mostly quiet and didn't smile easily. Their clothes were mostly drab. About the only more lively spots in Moscow were the American embassy and the construction of the first McDonald's Restaurant in the U.S.S.R. The golden arches had just gone up and we were told that the restaurant staff was being trained in Canada. Life at the time appeared to be extremely difficult for the Russian people. Some foods were scarce. Coffee was in very short supply.

On three different occasions, we were fortunate to be invited to the Holy Land by the Israeli Government. There was so much to see in Israel, from the modern city of Tel-Aviv to the ancient city of Jericho. In Bethlehem, we visited the Church of the Nativity, Jesus' birthplace. We also visited the Church of the Holy Sepulcher. Our itinerary took us to the Sea of Galilee, the River Jordan and the Dead Sea. In Jerusalem, we stood by the Wailing Wall and visited the Dome

of the Rock. Our experience visiting the Masada was quite
interesting. We learned that at one time, the Masada was a
favorite hideaway for King Herod.

In the Golan Heights, we stayed overnight at a kibbutz
(communal farm) named Cohen and Ayala. We were told that
Ayala in Hebrew meant "gazelle." Not too much time was
spent in the Gaza Strip. In the evenings, different Israeli leaders spoke to our group. One evening, General Moshe Dayan
explained to us why he felt the U.S. had lost the struggle in
Vietnam. He told us that in order to be successful in an armed
conflict, three very necessary components must be present: 1)
we must have strong, bright, young fighting men and women,
2) we must provide them with the most modern fighting equipment available and 3) we must have a cause. Americans, he
said, had strong, bright young men and women fighting with
the best equipment, but they did not have a good enough or
well-defined cause in Vietnam.

The subject of water is a daily issue with the Israeli officials. The use of drip water irrigation is more widely used there
than in any other country I visited. It has allowed their desert
to bloom. They refer to it as, "Shrinking the desert."

In Japan, I was impressed with the transportation system. In one day, we rode the subway, a bus, a boat and a high-
speed train. Irene and I took a tourist bus up Mt. Fuji as far as
we could. Mt. Fuji was a reference point for U.S. Airmen during WW II. We also went up the Tokyo Tower, giving us a
breathtaking view of Tokyo Bay.

Tokyo had few areas to park a car. People whose jobs
are located downtown, generally take taxicabs to work. There
was always a cab crunch at peak hours during our visit. Despite
the high population density, the Japanese people were very
polite. The city streets were clean and void of graffiti. The
gardens and parks were beautiful.

Some of our most enjoyable travels were personal trips

Irene and I took with George and Dee Borba to attend USC versus Notre Dame football games at South Bend, Indiana. Irene and I have always been faithful (rabid) supporters of the "SC Trojans" while George and Dee were equally supportive of the "Fighting Irish." Flying to chilly and windy Chicago and making the drive to Knute Rockne Stadium in Indiana was always a thrill. As a child, I never dreamed I would have ever had such an opportunity nor that I would ever hear the Notre Dame band play the USC Fight Song, of all places, on the steps of the Library of the Notre Dame Campus. On that campus, we witnessed a fervor for football seldom demonstrated any-where else. Admittedly, there were those sad occasions when I cried all the way home as a result of the game's final score. Still, the experiences are unforgettable. "FIGHT ON!"

This is a good opportunity to tell you about five class-mates who graduated from Chino High School with me and to the best of my knowledge still live in Chino. They are Patty Hodson Allen, Joe Jertberg, Christine Campos Martinez, Verne Berryman and Fred Decker. Patty Hodson married another classmate, Doyle Allen. He passed away in 2002. Doyle was a WWII veteran and served under General Patton in Europe. Patty is a retired schoolteacher from the Chino Unified School District. Joe Jertberg joined the Navy after attending Chaffey College and served in the South Pacific during WWII. Joe is a successful strawberry grower with fields located throughout southern California. Christine also retired as a school teacher from Chino Unified School District. She had also been a "D" Street School classmate of mine. Verne Berryman was a wide receiver with the Chino Cowboys football team and a great run-ner on the Chino High track team. Verne served as a Navy pilot in both WWII and the Korean conflict. He retired after a successful career with the Gas Company. Verne and I often enjoy a cup of coffee at one of our favorite local restaurants. Fred Decker served during WWII with the 8th Air Force in the

European theater of war. He retired from the commercial
building construction business.

I am deeply honored by the fact that during my tenure
as an elected official, I was a recipient of numerous awards and
honors by well-respected organizations. It was a humbling
experience to be named "Legislator of the Year" by the League
of California Cities, the Southern California Metropolitan
Water District, the Association of California Water Agencies
(ACWA), the American Public Works Association - San
Bernardino/Riverside Branch, the American Legion of
California, the California State Veterans of Foreign Wars and
the AM-Vets. Other awards included the "Inaugural Lifetime
Achievement in Water Resources Award" given by the Water
Resources Institute at California State University at San
Bernardino and the "Southern California Water Council's
Wieder Leadership Award."

In 1985, the Inland Empire Council of Boy Scouts of
America honored me as the "Special Jubilee Year Distinguished
Citizen." In 1988, California State Polytechnic University
Chapter of Phi Kappa Phi honored me for my "Statesmanship
in Working Towards Providing a Stable Economy in the Area
of Labor and Management." San Bernardino County named a
park in Bloomington after me in 1983. In 1981, the City of
Rialto named one of its streets, "Ayala Drive." I was especially
pleased when I was named "Citizen of the Year" by my hometown of Chino. Chino's joint elementary schools also awarded
me an Honorary Life Membership Award. In 1982, Chino City
officials named the now 140-acre community park on the corner of Edison and Central Avenues in Chino, "The Ruben S.
Ayala Park." It's a beautiful sprawling park with soccer and
baseball fields, playgrounds, picnic areas, a skate park, the
YMCA, a golf driving range wand batting cages. City officials
have plans to significantly further enhance the park.

In November 1987, the City of Chino celebrated the

city's Centennial Birthday with a parade. I was honored to be named the parade's Grand Marshal. George Putnam, a television news personality led the Equestrian units. Mr. Putnam has been a long-time citizen and genuine credit to our community. According to the Chino Champion, the parade lasted almost three hours with over 4,000 participants. The parade was also attended by John Gird, 82 at the time. John was the nephew of Richard Gird, one of Chino's principal pioneer founders.

In 1986, the Chino Unified School Board conferred upon me and my family one of the highest honors possible by naming its new high school, the "Ruben S. Ayala High School." I don't believe a higher honor can be bestowed upon an individual than to name an institution of learning after that person. My family and I were overwhelmed by such a unique and distinguished honor. We are most appreciative of then Chino School Board President, Harold Nelms and Board members Dena Beno, Earl Owens and Dona Silva.

My great appreciation notwithstanding, I am also aware that there were some in the community who opposed naming the new high school after me. They said that it had nothing to do with their opinion of me, but they didn't approve of schools being named after politicians. Others believed that the name of their new high school should reflect the geography of the area rather than any individual. Others believed that if a new school was to be named after an individual that it shouldn't be named after a living person.

Recently, I attended Ayala's Cross-Country Team Awards Dinner. I was told that many who had opposed naming the high school after me were now pleased with the results. I have to say that I, too, am gratified, especially as students at Ayala High have excelled in various fields, such as academics, athletics, band, performing arts, etc. It's my understanding that Ayala's API (Academic Performance Index) score increased from 688 to 750 from year 2000 to 2003. I am told that at the

time, 750 was the highest API score a high school had ever
attained in San Bernardino County. Ayala's Band and Choir
performing groups have won numerous State and National
Awards. Most recently, the Ayala Water Polo team won its first
Division 5 CIF Championship against rival Damien High
School. The Ayala Bulldogs have been the Sierra League
Champions in each of the following sports: Baseball, Boys and
Girls Basketball, Boys and Girls Cross Country, Football, Golf,
Boys and Girls Soccer, Softball, Boys and Girls Swimming,
Boys and Girls Tennis, Boys and Girls Track and Field,
Volleyball, Boys and Girls Water Polo and Wrestling. In all,
Ayala High offers 15 different sports programs and 35 clubs to
provide a complete educational experience for its well-diversi-
fied student body. My genuine respect to Dr. Glenna Ramsay,
Ayala's founding Principal, for the tone and example of excellence she first established. My hat's off to Principal Michael
Hunkins, for contributing to Ayala's continuing improvement
and to Principal Dennis Gideon for his energy and commitment to educating our youth. And, I want to thank all of the
administrators, teachers, support personnel, coaches, parents
and students who have individually and collectively made Ayala
High School what it is today. Thank you for your ongoing
commitment to excellence.

Our life experiences have been most gratifying and ful-
filling to Irene and me and to our family. Serving 43 years in
public office made it possible for us to help many people in all
kinds of circumstances. That's what we've liked doing the
most, helping people better help themselves. I believe that's
what governments and communities should do. I have been
blessed with more opportunities in my life's journey than I ever
dared dream of when I was attending the old "D" Street
School in the Chino Barrio. Recently, while waiting for Irene to
do some shopping at the Montclair Plaza, I ran into an Iwo
Jima, Purple Heart Marine Corps veteran. Jim is now an

attorney/building contractor and lives in Highland, California. We reminisced and compared notes regarding our postwar experiences. On parting, we shook hands and he said, "Senator, you served your school district, your city, your county, your state and your country. And you did it well." Coming from a fellow Marine, his words were very much appreciated.

In retrospect, I believe my decision to enter public service grew out of my sincere desire to serve people on a larger scale rather than solely work for a corporation. I suppose that my self-confidence and the fact that I enjoyed rising to a challenge had something to do with it, as well.

In early July of 2002, I received a phone call from a dear family friend and long time supporter, Vera Cattle. Vera's husband, the late Howard Cattle, was a personal friend and former Chino Mayor. He had a long history of civic involvement and contribution to the community. An elementary school in the Chino Valley Unified School District has been named in his honor, Howard Cattle Elementary School.

Vera's call was in regard to a surprise she had for Irene and me. She invited us over to her home to present it to us. We were happy to oblige. Vera and her granddaughter, Dawnnelle Roberts, warmly greeted us at the door.

Once seated, Vera presented us with three large scrap books filled with newspaper clippings dating all the way back to my first election to the school board. Vera had accumulated this collection throughout my entire 43 year career in public office. I was flabbergasted.

Irene and I could not adequately thank Vera and her family for this tremedous collection now so valuable to us. Vera's daughter, Marcia Roth, had done a lot of the preparation of the scrapbooks and deserves special thanks for the many hours she dedicated to this project. Irene and I were and still are overwhelmed by the thoughtfullness demonstrated by the Cattle Family. We have spent many hours reading and studying the articles. The articles have also been very helpful in preparing the manuscript for this book. Thank you, Vera and your family for caring so much! Your work will be kept at the Ruben S. Ayala Research Center at Ayala High School for the benefit of students and others.

On March 6, 2003, I celebrated my 81st birthday with my family. My granddaughters, Sarah and Amy, called me in the morning and sang, "Happy Birthday!" That evening they called again to wish me a happy birthday. When I asked them why they were so thoughtful to call me twice in one day to wish me a happy birthday, without hesitation, they responded, "Because you are special!" All of the honors of the world can't compare to the honor I felt at that moment. To Danielle, Sarah, Amy and to all my family and friends, "I think you're special, too!"

"Up From Second Street"   Ruben S. Ayala

CHAPTER TWELVE

WHAT'S IN A NAME?

While attending a Western States Water Council Meeting in Salt Lake City, Utah, Irene and I decided to visit the Mormon Church's Genealogical Society Library. We were told it was the largest collection of genealogical resources in the world. We thought that it would be fun just to watch people research their family's lineage. But once there, it appeared to be so fascinating, we decided to give it a try. We did and we got hooked! We started out on the first floor with known ancestors. Then we moved on to the second floor, where we tracked down additional information regarding our family tree through an impressive network of computers. After exhausting our search there, we moved on to the third floor. We just kept going until we finally ran into a dead end. At that point, we were able to trace the Ayala side of the family to the Spanish Pyrenees in the Basque Province. Spain had invaded Mexico in 1519 and ruled it until 1810. Perhaps our ancestors were part of the Spanish migration to Mexico that followed.

A San Bernardino Basque Priest once told me that Ayala in Basque referred to "rolling hills." And, of course, there is the French champagne named Ayala Champagne. In Israel, the Chief Justice of the Supreme Court told our group that Ayala in Hebrew meant "gazelle." There is an Ayala Freeway in the City of Manila in the Philippine Islands.

"Up From Second Street"   Ruben S. Ayala

California history will tell you that a young naval officer with the Spanish Armada, named Juan Bautista De Ayala, was in charge of one of the first ships to sail into San Francisco Bay. This young officer is given credit for surveying Angel and Alcatraz Islands. Angel Island was once a major immigration station, as well as an army base on the West Coast during the Civil War. Today, the island is a tourist attraction with a cove called "Ayala Cove." And of course, we have all heard of the famous prison on Alcatraz Island. Finally, former Assemblyman Bill McVittie brought from Spain a large poster featuring a famous bullfighter named - Ruben Ayala.

When I first hear the name, "*Ayala*," I don't immediately think of any of the previously mentioned references. Rather, I first think of my wife, Irene. Then I think of my father, Mauricio and my mother, Herminia. Of course, I quickly remember my paternal grandparents, Cesario and Inez, my Aunt Esther and my siblings, Maury, Susie, Stella and Rosina. As I consider the tremendous gratitude I feel for all of them, I can't help but think of my sons, Bud, Maurice and Gary and Bud's wife, Jeanne. Finally, I think of my precious granddaughters, Danielle, Sarah and Amy. Then after a brief pause, I think to myself,

"Ayala, I love that name! It reminds me of the people I love so dearly ... my family."

INDEX

<u>NOTES</u>

<u>NOTES</u>

<u>NOTES</u>

NOTES

<u>NOTES</u>

<u>NOTES</u>